Suicide Charlie

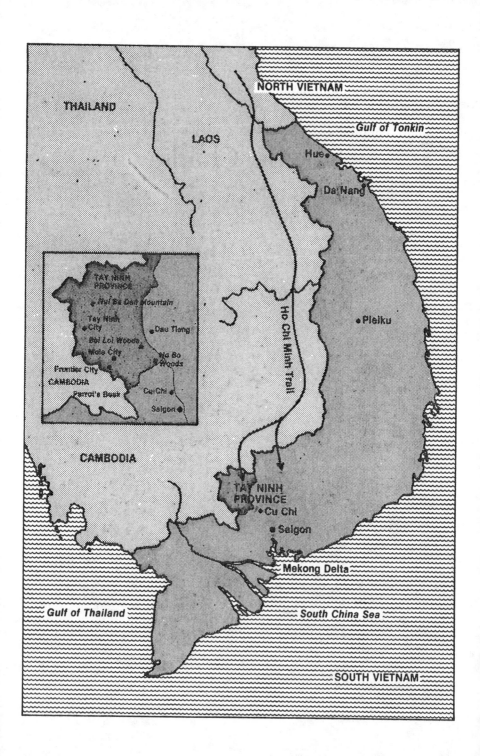

Suicide Charlie
A Vietnam War Story

Norman L. Russell

PRAEGER

Westport, Connecticut
London

ISBN: 0–275–94521–9

First published in 1993

Praeger Publishers, 88 Post Road West, Westport, CT 06881
An imprint of Greenwood Publishing Group, Inc.

Printed in the United States of America

To the men of Charlie Company, 4th Bn. 9th Inf. Bde.,
25th Infantry Division (U.S. Army), as well as those of the 207th
Regiment, 9th Army (NVA), and, most especially, to a boy whose name
I will never know. May we all find peace.

Contents

Acknowledgments

As with any creative work, this book did not spring forth fully grown from the head of the author. Three World War II veterans were of great assistance in its development: Robert G. Tucker, whose genius as a teacher of creative writing was surpassed only by his kindness and generosity; John M. Garber, who nurtured my ambition simply by taking it seriously when few others did; and J. William "Bill" Hoth, whose hidden hand can be found throughout the manuscript. I would also like to thank Clark Dougan for his interest and encouragement, as well as my wife, Sharon J. Zingler, without whose perspectives and tolerance *Suicide Charlie* might never have been written.

Suicide Charlie

1

Getting Acquainted

The dark comes. It is the greatest enemy.

Dark is the haunting ground of terror. It presses into our skin until we, it, everything, is black.

It is a black that lives, moves, a creature of shadow and sound.

The veterans speak of the night as if it were a sentient being, a huge ocean beast that swallows us whole at sunset, then spews us back out at dawn. From our raft of a base camp we poke and prod the belly of night, sending out small groups of men to penetrate the darkness, scouts who study it with instruments: starlight scopes and infrared receivers.

They stare into the darkness through the hollow eyes of mystics seeking revelation. They startle it with parachute flares that reflect the ribs of the sky in a brilliant flash of white phosphorous. Spent, the dangling flares splutter earthward, tiny dying suns that flicker and fail, creating last images as spasmodic and distorted as a madman's laughter.

The boom-boom girls back at the barter point clutched at their breasts and wailed like mourners at a mass funeral as we loaded onto choppers and lifted skyward. The clever boys in ragged shorts and sandals packed their bicycles with canned soda and beer and pedaled furiously, as if racing the choppers to our next destination.

Deep in enemy territory, the choppers hugged the ground so tightly that they had to jump over tree lines. I felt as though I were lost inside an Escher painting, not knowing what was up, what was down, where the sky ended and the earth began. We jerked through space with our legs dangling from open doors and the wind ripping at our camouflage-colored fatigue pants. Bits of flesh sprayed across us as the furious blades chopped through a startled flock of birds.

We came in low, low and fast, because the landing zone might be hot. The choppers hovered inches above the roiling elephant grass that stood tall as a man and was sharp as knives when we leaped into it. It sliced our hands and faces as we crabwalked beneath our heavy packs, scurrying towards a small clearing where combat patrol base "Mole City" was to be built.

Back home it was wintertime, the ground covered with snow. Here, on the Tay Ninh–Cambodian border, it was dry season, the dusty earth hard as brick beneath the powdery surface. With pickax and shovel we attacked the red clay, pounding out trenches and bunkers, filling sandbags and layering them atop corrugated strips of metal—willing an underground fortress out of the mean earth.

I was a fucking new guy, an FNG the veterans said, greener than my olive-drab T-shirt. My skin was still pink beneath the burning tropical sun. But, quickly, the dust sifted down into my pores and I darkened into the night that settled like a giant black shroud across our unfinished base camp.

Three weeks earlier I had been walking down Mill Street in the small Western Massachusetts town of Greenfield, kicking at clumps of leaves that littered the sidewalk in the damp cold evening, on my way to visit my father. The next day I would be catching a plane for Travis Air Force Base in Oakland, California, where my name was on a manifest for Vietnam.

The skeletons of things come out in the fall in New England. Surrounded by the bare bones of trees, naked shrubs, and rain-splattered asphalt, it was hard to shake a feeling that I wouldn't make it back.

My father fought in World War II, but he never told me about it. Haunted by memories, disappointed by a postwar reality that did not match his overseas dreams, he hanged himself in the attic nine months after I was born.

My older brothers remembered him as a fading shadow who sat, day after day, in a chair in the corner of the living room until he made that terrible journey up the narrow stairway.

As I made my solitary trek along the darkened streets of what had been his hometown too, and up the steep curve of Wisdom Way to the Green River Cemetery where he is buried, my thoughts centered on the journey that lay before me.

The future is a vanishing point that disappears into the present. I stood before his grave, moonlight sifting through the swirling clouds and breaking across the simple granite headstone that marked his passage into mystery, and it seemed as if my life had led inevitably to this moment.

Questions. I had so many to ask him. Questions without answers, feelings without form. I wanted to speak to him but I couldn't find the words. He'd left me so little to go on.

Instead, I just stood in the moonlight, wondering why.

I felt totally unprepared for what would come next. Eighteen weeks is not much time to get ready for war. I had never owned a gun, never hunted. I'd had no father against whom I could test my strength and will as sons so often do, to teach me the lessons that only a father can teach. The army said that I was a soldier, a marksman with an M-16, but I knew better.

Finally, shaking from the cold, I said—more to myself than to him— "Well, Dad, I guess this is where it all starts." I turned on my heel, already unconsciously military in my mannerisms, and marched slowly back down the hill.

The second night. The dark slouches in on huge velvet haunches and hunkers down upon Mole City. Its sable mane ripples in the gentle breeze and flows softly across the jungle. The tropical night clasps us in its sticky paws, playing with our minds like a cat does its prey, teasing us, so certain of its kill.

It is border darkness, ancient as time, the primordial night from which all things are formed. The darkness of the great void, of the tiny spaces between atoms and the vast reaches between galaxies.

Border darkness. It is a darkness so deep that I hold it in my hand and feel weight, I can squeeze it in my fist and give it shape. I can blow on it and feel its heat.

The night is so real that I can give it a name. The name is Terror.

All through that first day, and the second and the third, we chopped at the hard soil, burrowing into the ground with the instinctive determination of dung beetles. Charlie Company, 4th of the 9th, was the name of my unit. Suicide Charlie, more commonly. A company of survivors. They'd come by their name honestly. Three weeks before, they had lost most of their comrades in an ambush. It wasn't the first time. We were the replacements for dead men.

I was now a Manchu, as the companies of the 9th Battalion are known. My outfit earned its battle name during the Boxer Rebellion that took place in China at the turn of the century when a secret society of rebels had attempted to drive the foreigners back over the ocean. They had failed, but the spirit of resistance lived on.

I had received my assignment to Charlie Company back in Cu Chi, headquarters for the 25th Division, my first stop on the way to the field after spending a night or two at the Bien Hoa "Repo Depot" (for repositioning). While I was standing in line waiting for equipment, a clerk asked me if I could type. Apparently, he had noticed the civilian occupation of newspaper reporter listed in my personnel file. Though I had barely graduated from the hunt-and-peck school during my year at the Greenfield *Recorder*, I was quick with a yes, and he told me to step out of line.

"I might be able to do something for you," he said. "I'll have to check with the first sergeant. Wait here and I'll be back in about fifteen minutes."

He went off to see about changing my orders. I took a seat and basked in the glower of the envious stares of the other new guys as I contemplated the glorious prospect of life in the rear. The men back at the office had been right, I decided. The army had changed.

True to his word, the clerk returned in about a quarter of an hour only to inform me that my reprieve had been short lived. Suicide Charlie was too desperate for men. The first sergeant had told him that no exception could be made for anyone assigned to the Manchus.

"If you'd come through yesterday, or tomorrow, . . ." he said, perhaps with a trace of pity.

So I stepped back into line, just another grunt working his way to the front. It took a few more days to get there.

During the time I spent in Cu Chi, I got to know the rear-echelon motherfuckers (REMs) real well. They'd stop me in the street, knowing I was an FNG by my white skin and shiny boots, and ask me what unit I had been assigned to. When I answered that it was Charlie Company, 4th of the 9th, they'd shake their heads and smile knowingly.

"Suicide Charlie," they'd say. "You're dead right now, motherfucker."

Then they'd call over their friends, shouting, "Hey, catch a load of this dude. Dead meat."

Their buddies would come up to me, smirking that same dumb smile—one that reminded me of a fellow I met in San Francisco my last night in the States.

A few guys split to Saigon, risking court-martials rather than joining up with Suicide Charlie. Me, I grabbed my gear and headed for the airstrip the moment my orders came down. I was tired of being treated like a freak by strangers.

I flew from Cu Chi to Dau Tieng on an old C-47 cargo plane that rattled and shook like a drunk with DTs. Rough as the flight was, the landing was even hairier. The tarmac at Dau Tieng was pockmarked with craters, and the plane lurched and swayed as the pilot swerved to avoid them.

Dau Tieng was a relic of more than twenty years of war. First the French, now the Americans, I thought as I lugged my duffel bag over to an adobe terminal that was riddled with bullet holes.

Our stay at the base was short, just long enough to shower and get a restless night's sleep in wooden barracks that appeared to offer little protection in the case of a mortar attack. The next morning we loaded onto deuce-and-a-halfs (2½-ton trucks) that were piled high with gear, munitions, and New Guys.

Bouncing along on the dusty track I got my first good look at the Vietnamese countryside. The sky was a clear tropical blue as we passed lush expanses of rubber trees and rice paddies. The land was as flat as the American Midwest.

Riding with me was a fellow named Mike Pincush, who shared my assignment as an ammo bearer in Suicide Charlie's heavy weapons platoon. Two of our new squad mates, Stan and Kumo, met us at the bunker line when our convoy rolled into their base camp. They showed us to our bunker where we met Francis, who had arrived a week earlier, and Harry, our squad leader.

Introductions were brief and comprehensive. Harry's father owned a mining business in Appalachia. He (Harry) was a short-timer with less than a month left in-country. Kumo was a native Hawaiian and he didn't care much for haoles, or mainlanders. Stan came from Rockford, Illinois. He'd once dated Miss America, before she won her crown, and he had a picture to prove it. Said they'd had a personality clash. Francis came from a town in Florida so small I had never heard of it. He called gooks "goops," and thought Buck Owens was better than the Beatles. Pincush was an accountant who looked sort of like Richard Nixon. Didn't know a thing, just like me. Strangers since birth, we were now comrades-in-arms.

The dark comes. It is the fourth night. Mole City squats within the dense vegetation nearly invisible to the uninformed eye. The weight of anticipation lies heavy on the crescent of bunkers where Suicide Charlie's troopers crouch, tensely scanning a darkness so thick we can almost part it like water.

As we watch, the night begins to coalesce. It takes form in dim and ill-defined shapes and sounds: the scuffling of sandal-clad feet, and words whispered in a foreign tongue. Our radios crackle with messages from listening posts out beyond the wire.

"We've got movement," they report.

A hushed message flows across the base camp, passed from bunker to bunker. Something is out there. Something is moving.

The night is alive.

Our bladders constrict and we urinate into tin cans, afraid to stray far from our bunkers. Our bodies tremble involuntarily as if the night were bitterly cold.

Stillness. The stillness of absolute zero. Of death. Of bodies crumbling into dust. We can feel our bodies disintegrating. The dark is taking us in, absorbing us into its seamless fabric. We want to dissolve into dark, to become invisible, formless, and invulnerable.

The night moves.

With the ferocity of a giant beast suddenly enraged, it roars, spitting fire and light. Enemy rockets and mortars crash into Mole City. The earth shakes with their impact, and geysers of molten steel eject cascades of shimmering flame into the air. Shrapnel splatters around us, hissing and steaming as it cuts into the ground. Explosions rip apart the night and we flee from the light into darkness, crawling into our bunkers and waiting in huddled desperation as miniature volcanoes erupt all across the base camp and the earth ripples and sways.

Under the cover of the barrage, North Vietnamese soldiers rush toward Mole City, stopped only by the spirals of razor-edged concertina wire that ring our encampment. At such a close distance the same explosions that pin us in our bunkers imperil them as well, and the enemy gunners lift their fire.

Harry says it's time to go back outside.

We scurry out from our bunker and, for a moment, it is absolutely silent. It is the quiet before the thunderclap, the cut before the pain. Time is suspended as we wait for the ground attack; then the enemy opens fire and eternity begins.

Green tracers slice through the darkness as hundreds of AK-47s all fire at once. The air screams like a wounded man. Shrieking projectiles slam into sandbags, dirt, and bodies, ripping apart the earth and sky as if they, too, were made of flesh.

I crouch behind the parapet, transfixed by the bloodcry of the dark that comes from beyond the grave. It calls to an ancient tribal memory buried deep in my soul.

It is the voice of the Devil, screaming.
Instinctively, I reach for my rifle.
It is time we made our acquaintance, the Devil and I.
I am an infantryman now.

2

Code of Silence

The Halifax Gorge: green water, cold and deep, Vermont granite, slick and worn.

From high up on Route 8a, we can hear the roar of the falls. Grabbing our towels, my friends and I jump the guardrail and jog eagerly down the dirt path to the cool moist chasm where the Cold River cascades into a deep swimming hole.

Stubborn trees cling to the steep hillside and we leap across their thick roots that lie gnarled and twisted as an old man's fingers. Grabbing at saplings and branches to steady our balance, we slip-slide along the mud-slickened trail, then stagger out onto the open rocks that brace the ancient stream.

A billowing mist washes across our sweaty bodies as we strip naked and pick our way to the water's edge. Jon and Rick close behind me, I dive through the shimmering spray and plunge deep into the velvet depths beneath the waterfall.

Thrusting back to the surface, I gasp for air amid the churning froth. With quick sure strokes I swim out into the middle of the glacial pool and flip over on my back. Floating with the current, I glide along, pushed downstream to where a beaver family is busily repairing its dam. When I float too close, the stone walls echo with the sharp report of the elder beaver slamming his tail against the water in warning.

Not wishing to disturb the rightful residents, I swim over to the bank and climb onto the flat warm rocks. Lying naked in the sun, my skin sleek and pink, I feel ancient, reptilian, as the hot rays burrow into my tight cold flesh.

From the rocks above, the voices of my friends drift past me. They are talking about the War—a war many say will soon be over and that I had hoped to avoid. There are rumors of peace, but it is too late for me. I passed my draft physical in April and it is now early June. My induction date is only two weeks away.

Jon slides down to my side. He's a thoughtful kid with long brown hair that's soon to be shorn. He has enlisted in the navy to avoid the draft and will be shipping out in a few days.

"What are you going to do, Norm?" he asks, his soft blue eyes searching mine for an answer. "Go to Canada? Go to jail?"

His real question goes unspoken, but I know what he's thinking. It's been on all of our minds. Do I think that I could kill?

For that question, I have no answer. Shrugging my shoulders, I stand and stretch. Walking slowly to the edge, I plunge back into the pool and swim to the other side. Pulling myself out of the water, I clamber up the steep slope to the peak of a ledge that juts out nearly forty feet above the pool. I hear the voices of Jon and Rick rising up around me.

"C'mon, dive," they shout, knowing I have never dared to before. "You can do it."

Defiantly, I stand at the very top of the gorge, high above the dark stream. I want to make this one dive to hold in my memory long after I have said goodbye.

Looking down, I see the sky reflected in the opaque pool. Blue, with a few clouds, white and puffy, and a solitary figure, alone among the pines. Fear snaps at me, and my stomach churns as if I have swallowed a vat of wriggling snakes. I could just walk away; there is a path that leads to a shallow fording spot above the falls. But this time I won't let myself do it.

I take a deep breath and hold it, bending my knees, my arms outstretched. Leaping. A true, perfect dive from high above the rocks, arching through the crystalline air and down, down, deep into the pure embracing water.

Hard choices, the spring of 1968. Jail, Canada, or war. For working-class kids like me who came of age in the late sixties, the draft was a fact of life as inevitable as acne and sexual anxiety.

It dominated our consciousness in a subliminal kind of way, always flitting around the edges of awareness, an apparitional representation of the dull adult world that occasionally intruded into our otherwise self-contained existences.

We all hoped that, if we waited long enough, it would just go away. But it didn't. The best poet in my high school class had written a poem entitled "1965–66." It was all about the Vietnam War, and I had used it to lead off the literary magazine I edited. It was now two years later and the war showed little sign of abatement.

We were like the kids who got out of high school after Pearl Harbor—with one big difference. Nobody I knew wanted to serve, and those that could were getting out any way possible.

College was the big out. A 2-S deferment meant four years of fraternity parties and lecture halls instead of body bags, firefights, and fear. All it took was the money and inclination to go to school. I had neither.

With eight kids and no dad, my family had been very poor. Those were the days before AFDC and food stamps, and we ate a lot of beans. Our house in Montague, Massachusetts, was built before the American Revolution, and it showed its age. A slab wood burner in the dirt basement belched smoke and fire all winter. The plumbing always froze during the cold weather, and the shallow well went dry every summer.

My father's absence hung over the family like a shadow. My mother never mentioned him, and neither did my brothers and sisters. In the mystery that surrounded a father who, for me, had never existed, I created a godlike being. The few times I uttered the word "Dad" my voice quavered and broke as it might for an iconoclastic Jew speaking the name of Yahweh.

I was seven or eight years old before I learned that he had committed suicide. A kid down the road told me. Said he'd hanged himself with a coat hanger. That didn't seem possible, but the image stuck with me. At night when I climbed the narrow back stairway to my bedroom, I often sensed that there was a man up there and that, just as I made it to the top and all the ghosts and monsters of childish fantasy vanished, I'd open the wrong door and see his body swinging limply, the rafters creaking from its weight.

The man in the attic haunted my childhood in less figurative ways as well. His legacies included poverty and the shroud of shame that falls across the shoulders of the survivors of suicides. There was also the simple incompleteness of being that comes from growing up in a fatherless home. It is hard for a boy to become a man without a role model to follow.

Adolescence is treacherous enough in the healthiest of households. My problems were compounded by the atmosphere of despair in which I was raised and the difficulty of adjusting to a new social environment when my family moved to Florida just as I was entering the eighth grade. Florida meant football, money, and tanned bodies. Everybody seemed rich, by my standards, with new clothes, new cars, and new houses.

After the variety of New England's natural surroundings, I felt like I was living inside a two-dimensional universe. It was too hot, too flat, and too gray. Fortunately, we went back up North every summer, where I picked shade tobacco, kept up old friendships, and ached inside each September as we made the long drive down Route 301. Late at night, as we passed through the swamps and scrub pines of South Carolina and Georgia, I listened to radio WBZ-Boston until it faded into static. I felt as if I, too, were fading out, my northern me disintegrating as the miles drifted. Gospel music replaced rock'n'roll on the airwaves and, with it, my southern self gradually resubstantiated.

School was okay until my senior year. Then the New Order arrived, in the form of a reactionary principal who took an immediate disliking to me.

It was my hair that did me in.

I had bangs that fell across my forehead—a radical style in the mid-sixties. I had recently discovered girls and thought bangs made me look sexy, at least compared to the crew cut that had led to my gaining the nickname "Fish."

The new principal saw matters differently. To him, my Beatle haircut was a sign of poor moral character. Though I kept the locks the requisite two finger widths above my eyebrows, he decided to make an example out of me. Sympathetic teachers told me that he had vowed to get me expelled, but he never found sufficient grounds to do so. Instead, he settled for making my school life as miserable as possible.

One day I was called to the office and the school secretary handed me a plaque citing me as an Outstanding Scholar of Pinellas County. It turned out that they had held a recognition dinner the night before, but I had not been invited. Another time, a student aide told me that she overheard the principal on the phone saying that he could not recommend me for a certain college scholarship. He even tried to keep my picture out of the class yearbook, but the staff rebelled and my photo remained in, bangs and all.

I didn't fully understand the social context of my situation, but it was directly related to the war in Vietnam. As more and more troops were shipped overseas, the nation was splitting into opposing camps, pro- and anti-war. Symbols became all important. While young men died from bullets and booby traps in the jungles and rice paddies of Southeast Asia, a shadow war was fought in the United States in which the opposing armies were identified by their styles of dress, grooming, and speech.

It was the hips against the straights, the Movement against the War, the young against the old. Instinctively, I had sided with the forces of rebellion. When my Senior Year in Hell was over, I headed straight back to New England, where civic dissent has maintained a long and cherished tradition dating back to the days of Daniel Shays' Rebellion.

I stepped off the bus in Greenfield, seventeen years old and without an inkling of what to do next but, as I walked down Main Street, I felt good. I knew that I was home.

After the hassles of my senior year, the idea of attending college right off didn't hold much attraction. I had neither the money nor the inclination. My plan was to work for a year and save up as much as I could, and then go to school. But when I turned eighteen the summer after graduation and told the draft board of my plans, they said no way, any break in schooling terminated the deferment. It didn't seem fair—but when had life ever been? So I did the only sensible thing. I signed up for a two-year hitch at the local community college.

I lasted only six weeks. Sitting in a classroom when I wanted to be out making my way in the world ran against my nature. The biggest problem, however, was lack of money. After tuition and books, what little money I had saved that summer working as a dishwasher was gone. My stomach often rumbled as I waited for the relief of sleep in my dingy, one-room apartment in a downtown tenement that stank of disease and the decaying dreams of the dying old men and women with whom I shared a sordid tub and toilet.

One of the reasons I had been drawn to Greenfield was that I had a romantic liaison with a girl named Kelly, whom I had met during my tobacco-picking days and with whom I maintained a long-distance relationship over the ensuing winters. The juvenile tragedy of our forced separations had inflamed our passions; once that was removed, however, our affair quickly deteriorated. Broke and disheartened, I bounced around from job to job until I landed the position at the *Recorder*.

Suddenly, for the first time in my life, I had money in my pocket, a nice apartment, and a flashy car—a bright red '61 Chevy convertible. For the next twelve months, life settled into a pleasant routine. During the day I pounded the sports beat, at night my friends would filter into my apartment and we'd hang out, drinking beer, listening to music, and occasionally smoking a little marijuana. When the weather was good, we went on big group picnics up in the hills or loaded into my convertible to cruise out to the Halifax Gorge to go skinny-dipping—another fine New England tradition.

The only disconcerting note to this otherwise near idyllic situation was the way guys started disappearing. The largest draft calls of the war came in the spring of 1968, shortly after the Tet Offensive that had rocked the United States when enemy forces managed to attack nearly every major city in South Vietnam and briefly fought their way into the American Embassy Compound in Saigon.

The Johnson administration may have been talking peace, but it was doing war. About 200,000 men were called up during the months of April, May, and June. A few of the guys enlisted to avoid infantry duty, but most of my friends took the straight shot: two years and out. Maybe.

They'd come home on leave after infantry training, hyper, weird-looking with shaved heads, smoke a lot of pot and drink a lot of beer. . . . Then they'd really disappear. Sometimes we took them to the airport; sometimes we just saw them off at the bus station, where we'd wave an American flag while Peter Pan Bus Lines, our local transport, carried them off on the first stage of their journey to a real life Never-Never Land.

All spring I tried to push my concerns about the draft out of my thoughts. Cruising out to the gorge, it was almost too easy to imagine that I lived in a more innocent time. Deep inside the Vermont country-side, the War held little meaning. The gorge had seen glaciers come and go. Dinosaur footprints are stamped all over northern New England. Sitting in the shade of the tall pines, watching the tumbling water, I could forget what it meant to turn nineteen and a half in the spring of 1968.

Once I received my induction notice, however, it was time to face the inevitable. I thought about Canada, but I'd have been a stranger there. Jail held no allure. CO status—that is, conscientious objection—didn't make sense for me, because I just didn't know if I truly was a pacifist. And there was only one way to find out.

I watched the carnage on the nightly news like most everyone else, and the sight of it sickened me. I had my doubts about the War, and I didn't want to go to some appendix-shaped country halfway around the world to be maimed, killed, or turned into a mental basket case because President Lyndon Johnson had an ego twice the size of Texas. But I couldn't duck out on my duty and let some other poor bastard go fight in my place just because I was scared.

The guys at the office must have seen it coming, too. Some of my co-workers were World War II veterans, but they kept it to themselves. There was a code of silence among the World War II vets to which those guys remained true. They may have had misgivings about the War—by then a lot of people did—but they never spoke to me about them. All they ever said was, "The army's changed, Norm. They'll make a newspa-per reporter out of you." I guess that was their way of easing their consciences. Or maybe they figured that they went through hell so why shouldn't I?

As my induction date neared, Kelly suddenly retook an interest in me. The drama of separation was upon us again. I hadn't seen much of her over the past year, and I took her renewed affection with a large grain of salt. Still, she embodied the sweet memory of first love, and the tragedy that was unfolding for me was very real, indeed. We spent a lot of time together during those last few weeks, and I was grateful for the attention.

I also felt a sudden interest in resolving the mystery of my father's death. One day near the end of my tenure at the paper, it occurred to me that his obituary was somewhere in an old issue of the *Recorder*. The archives were located upstairs in a wide room that was perpetually gloomy despite tall windows. A good cleaning would have brightened the place considerably, had anyone thought to wash the dusty panes. The air of neglect that marked the room was enhanced by the cracked plaster walls, whose coat of faded green paint had not been renewed for decades.

Yellowed copies of the paper were bound in huge leather-jacketed volumes about two feet wide and three feet long. Once a week it was my job to leaf through these Brobdingnagian tomes and pick out interesting sports reports from fifty, twenty-five, and ten years ago. This exercise in journalistic ritual allowed me to spend many a quiet afternoon reading through the old papers. I learned that sports reporting had changed a lot over the years, progressing from terse styleless game summaries in which players were noted by first initial and last name only, to the colorful "in-depth" pieces and personality profiles that gradually evolved during the fifties as sports became more and more of an American obsession and the sports section expanded from a few columns to the several pages I was required to help fill out every day.

Though I cared little if M. Kicktoe scored six points in some long-forgotten gridiron clash between the Powertown 11 and the Chair City Pigskinners, the details of daily life revealed through advertisements were fascinating to consider. A loaf of bread that cost a nickel in 1919 had crept up to a dime by the early forties and zoomed to a quarter by 1958. Ads for bars of laundry soap and scrub boards during the Great War transmogrified into barrel-shaped washers with ringers on top before World War II, then entered the modern era with efficient box-shaped Maytags when America entered its golden age of prosperity after winning the Big One.

The World War II editions were filled with the war. A full-page ad for war bonds startled and shocked me. It depicted a heinous Japanese soldier who looked more like a crawling insect than a human being. His forehead slashed by barbed wire and a bayonet clenched in his teeth, he was sneaking with murderous intent toward an innocent babe of a GI.

The contrast with the present was graphic. In the United States, it was our soldiers who were often vilified and the Viet Cong who were idealized. The uniform was far from being a cloak of honor, but was more a hair shirt disdained with scorn. Middle-class kids clung desperately to their 2-S student deferred status in colleges that sprang up almost overnight to service a vast body of nascent scholars academically inspired by an eager desire to avoid military service.

When I located my father's obituary, I was amazed to discover that at the time of his death he had been working in the typesetting department of the *Recorder*. No one had bothered to tell me. I also learned that he had served as an infantryman in World War II. It seemed almost as if my life had twisted back on his and our fates had become intertwined.

As I closed the pages that held the stark outline of my father's life, I felt like I now knew him a little better. I realized, of course, that I could never truly understand the man who had haunted my early years, but there was one thing he had experienced that perhaps I could share. We are drawn sometimes, almost as if by compulsion, to follow in the footsteps of our fathers. He had been an infantryman. I would be one, too.

3

Lost in the South

It's too damn hot. Fort Benning, Georgia-in-July hot. Red clay soil, hazy damp horse latitudes hot. My fatigues are so soaked through with sweat that they form an extra layer of skin. Olive-drab epidermis.

There're yards of agony between me and the end of the sand pit, and no oxygen left in my bloodstream. My lungs are breathing pain. My pulse is counting cadence and my heart is pumping double time.

"Russell, you dumb scumbagbastard, move your ass or we're gonna' carve it up and feed it to the hogs," my drill sergeant drawls with sadistic, sweet-toned menace. "Crawl, you lazy pink-assed Yankee. MOVE IT!"

I'm chewing sand in the low-crawl pit and I hate this redneck son of a bitch and everything he stands for. The heat, the hassling, the constant humiliation. I hate the sand that's grinding into my tender parts and the heat so fucking hot it could turn ice into steam in half a second. I hate the skinny bunk beds and the wooden barracks, the rubber-fried eggs and the goddamn soggy toast. I hate reveille, inspections, and jogging at 5 A.M., the hurry up and wait, the standing at attention and calling men "sir," the manual of arms and the classes on the U.S. Code of Military Justice.

But most of all, I hate this man standing at the end of the sand pit in his pressed starched fatigues, spit-shined boots, and ridiculous Smokey the Bear hat. I hate the smirk on his chubby, pork-fed face that tells me I'm an asshole if I can't make it to the end of the pit and spit on his boots like a real goddamned soldier.

And, because I hate him, I'm going to lift my arm and stretch it forward. I'm going to drag my leg through the clutching sand. I'm going to twist and crawl and strain and grunt and if I have to eat a ton of shit and swallow a gallon of piss to go that last fifteen feet, I'm going to do it, with a grin, just to show that smug black Cracker bastard that a white boy from the North can take the heat and the pain and the verbal abuse and anything else he's got to offer because I just love the look of disgust on his face when I stagger out of the pit and he says, "Trainee, I don't like the way you smile when you eat grits for breakfast. Get down and give me twenty."

I'm going to give him twenty-five.

I hitchhiked to Florida to get inducted because the Clearwater Selective Service Office didn't get my paperwork to Greenfield in time for me to go in up North. It's not that I was impatient to go into the service; it's just that I'd quit my job a few weeks earlier and I was down to my last fifty dollars. There wasn't much point to hanging around town an extra month, acting out the role of a latter-day Joe in Saul Bellow's *The Dangling Man*. Most of my friends had shipped out to Fort Dix in New Jersey, and the lease had expired on my apartment.

The sense of adventure appealed to me. A little Carl Sandburg in my life felt good right then, after a year behind a desk. As a Man of the Road, I figured to get a brief taste of America before I went off to fight for her.

My first ride came from a guy on his way to Bradley International, an airport just north of Hartford, Connecticut. He was a big guy, exuding muscle and power, who was on his way to Denver for a tryout with the Broncos. Much to my chagrin, he had received a medical exemption from the draft.

Now, I could understand that Joe Namath, the great New York Jets quarterback, might have a bit of trouble humping the boonies after nine knee operations. It probably took the best efforts of several paramedic teams to hold him together for one hour on the gridiron. But this guy was a middle linebacker.

I should have realized right then that I was being played for a sucker. Maybe I did. It didn't take a genius to figure out that something funny was going on when athletes like this guy were getting exemptions or, as was often the case, popping into convenient slots that just happened to open up in the local national guard unit while, for everyone else, the waiting list stretched off into infinity. It was a little late to make a U-turn in my life, however, so I just kept right on trucking down the coast.

Many of my rides came from draft-exempt young dudes who seemed to be making it big in the material world. They drove flashy cars, Bonnevilles and Toronados, and dressed in paisley shirts with fat Peter

Max splotches all over them. They boasted of their success in loud cheerful voices and, when I told them my story, they usually gave me a little money. I didn't mind. There were a lot of guys riding high in the war-inflated economy who liked to act hip and hang around the edges of the counterculture. I'd been one of them myself up until Uncle Sam got my number. If they bought me a meal or laid a few bills on me, that was okay. I'd helped out a couple of friends who were down on their luck when I was working at the *Recorder*.

As I made my way south from entrance ramp to entrance ramp (the Staties didn't like it if you hitched on the main highway), I fantasized about that mythical ride with a blonde in a white convertible who would offer one last taste of the good life to a soon-to-be-lonely GI, but it never materialized. Still, I made good time and saved my money until I reached the Carolinas. The interstate disappeared somewhere south of the Mason-Dixon line and, on the evening of the second day, I found myself stranded at a deserted crossroads outside of Fayetteville, North Carolina.

Under the flickering light of a tired humpbacked street lamp, I dropped down on my suitcase and waited for some traffic. Fortunately the night was warm and the mosquitoes weren't overly voracious. A few cars bumped past on the cratered asphalt, but the spirit of brotherly love apparently was lacking in the hearts of their drivers. As the night deepened, my young-man-off-to-the-army emotional patina began to tarnish, and I started to wonder if maybe I should have borrowed air fare instead of trusting my fate to the kindness of strangers.

Sitting on my battered bag, I remembered the first time I had hitch-hiked after moving to Florida. I was fourteen and had caught a ride from my sister to a friend's house for some sandlot football only to learn, after she left, that the game had been shifted to the high school playground. I started walking down the road and a young guy in an old coupe picked me up.

"Couldn't let a white boy walk alone through Danville," he said, explaining that "Danville" was the name white folks gave to the colored section of town.

The cheerful openness of his racism had startled me. I hadn't really thought about the fact that there were no black students at Largo Junior High. There hadn't been any at my school up North, either. That's because my hometown of Montague had been all white. But as we drove through Danville, I realized that there was a large black community, and learned from my benefactor that the blacks had their own school. For the first time in my life, the idea of segregation became real, and it didn't seem fair.

That same November, President John Kennedy had been shot in Dallas. As the special announcement crackled over the school's PA system, I heard scattered applause and remarks like "It serves the nigger-lover right."

Waiting beside the road, my schoolboy sense of isolation from being a Yankee boy in the land of Dixie came back to me. I began to wish that my hair was several inches shorter and my accent a whole lot softer. Tired as I was, I kept nodding off, only to be startled back awake as the occasional car or pickup truck blew past.

I was starting to wonder when some drunken good ol' boys might decide to have a little fun with me, when just then a '53 Olds pulled over. The driver, an itinerant musician, rolled down the window and demanded to see some cash before he'd unlock the door. I flashed my life's savings—about thirty bucks at that point—tossed my bag in the trunk, and hopped in beside him.

He told me the Olds had a quart-an-hour oil habit and gas mileage to make an Arab sheik smile. I could ride with him until we reached Florida or my money ran out, whichever came first. Early in the morning, we pulled into a peanut stand that doubled as a Sinclair station, the brand with a dinosaur for a logo. The arrow on the gas gauge was pointing toward the floor, so he decided to park until the proprietor arrived—at 6 A.M., according to the sign in the window.

The driver's name was Rick and he came from Savannah, but he wasn't going back there. He pulled out his saxophone and blew a few tunes, playing taps to the sunrise as we sat on the hood, sipped warm Dr. Pepper, and talked.

Rick didn't like southern men, northern women, blacks, or rock 'n' roll. He liked small nightclubs, steamed peanuts, and a man who could hold his liquor. He played show tunes in a combo that kept breaking up and then getting back together again. He had been in the army during the fifties, no war, played in the military band, and didn't like it. Thought I was nuts.

"You need a brain transplant, son," he told me, between notes of "You're in the Army Now." "You must be some kind of a factory reject that ain't been recalled yet. You better keep your eye on the papers. Those bureaucrats in Washington, D.C., are gonna' put a bulletin out on you."

He had some interesting ideas about the War and life in general.

"Vietnam, shit," he said. "There ain't no Vietnam. They gonna' send you to Utah, son. That's where the Vietnam War is being fought, just south of Mormon City. They're killing off all the young black dudes to keep the riots down. It's all part of the Minister's plan."

"Sure thing," I said, hopping down off the hood and slipping away into a clump of palmettos to pee. "Some minister."

"That's right, boy. The Minister of Misery, head bureaucrat in the Department of Payback. He's the guy in charge of the government. The fellow who sent you your greetings. Mark my words, son, he ain't done with you yet. The Minister's got plans for you. Five months' training and he's gonna' send your white ass right off to Utah. You been living good but payback's a bitch. And don't think you're gonna' get away now just because I'm telling you what's gonna' happen. The Minister keeps all the files."

His political views struck me as a bit paranoid, but I couldn't argue with his geography once he switched topics. He seemed to know every back road in Dixie country, and half the women who lived on them.

"They all nice women, son," he told me after I finished my business in the bushes. "Only the best. Southern women know how to treat a man like he's gonna' stay around awhile, even if he is just passing through. Ain't that right, honey?"

"Sure enough, fella'," answered a heavy-hipped woman who had slipped up on us unnoticed by me. "You sure blow some nice smoke on that horn of yours. You want some gas, or what?"

"Just fill it up, baby doll. Boy here's got the money. We've got miles to drive. He's got himself a date with good ol' Uncle Sam, and I don't want him to miss it. Gonna' go fight himself a war in Utah. Kill some niggas."

They both had themselves a good laugh while I blushed red as the swollen sun that was climbing over the sap-streaked pines. One of my precious tens filled the tank and restocked our supply of Dr. Pepper, then we headed back out on the highway. I bit my tongue and listened to the radio, worried that, if I said what I was feeling, Rick might dump me out on the road before my money ran out. The news was full of reports of racial unrest in some major northern cities and, after each bulletin, Rick would wink at me knowingly.

"You'll get your chance, son," he'd say, while I tried not to listen.

At first he must have taken my lack of response for agreement, but after a while he became suspicious.

"You ain't one of those there hippies?" he asked, after a particularly long spell of silence.

"Nope, a sportswriter," I answered. "At least, I used to be."

Sports is the universal language of the South—especially football—and we stuck to common ground the rest of the trip. Late that afternoon we hit more familiar territory: Central Florida. Outside of Orlando, he deposited me on the westbound ramp of I-4, aimed straight to the heart of Tampa Bay, penniless but proud to be there.

"Have a good time in Utah," Rick shouted as he rattled off for a club date somewhere down in Dade County. "Kill a couple for me."

"Eat shit," I hollered back, relieved to be free of his company. "I hope they get you first."

One ride later I was flying down the highway in a big black Lincoln Continental driven by the prototypical self-made American man, a self-professed millionaire who'd gone bankrupt three times before striking it rich with a chrome refinishing plant in Ybor City. He liked my story and bought me a thick juicy steak for dinner at the Spanish Gardens Restaurant. We toured his plant where blacks and chicanos were sweating over steamy vats of molten toxins so he could ride in style. He laid two tens in my palm and I walked over to the bus station, one transfer ticket away from home, my faith in my fellow man tested but found true.

The next morning I stepped over the line at the Clearwater induction center and boarded a bus back to Georgia. The future marines got off our bus in Jacksonville, Florida, to transfer to another bus. They were all the little guys, skinny, five and a half feet tall, shoulder high to the backs of the seats as they cockwalked down the isle for a honeymoon on Parris Island.

The rest of us rode on to Fort Benning, "Infantry Capital of the U.S. Army," as the sign at the gate proclaimed. The moment we got off the bus the drill-instructor sergeants—the DIs—were in our faces, screaming at us about how stupid, lazy, worthless, and ugly we were. They herded us into a big room where a gang of sadomasochistic barbers shaved our heads, wielding wide-angle shears with swift merciless strokes. When I looked in the mirror I had to admit that the DIs were right about one thing: I certainly was ugly. We all were.

Greasers, hippies, surfers, and Bubbas, we all looked like overgrown infants as we marched off to an auditorium for a battery of personality tests. I patted my scalp with tissue paper to stanch the bleeding, picked up a number-two lead pencil when the command was given, and studied the multiple choice questions. I considered trying to fudge the answers to fool the army into thinking that I was some sort of geeky nerd who couldn't be trusted to lace his boots straight so they wouldn't put me in the infantry.

To hell with it, I decided. Smarter guys than me had written the questions. I'd play it honest and take my chances. When I got to question #39 I had second thoughts. It read:

If you had the choice would you rather spend the afternoon——
A) In the library, researching a school paper, or;
B) Taking a hike in the woods.

(pick one)

It didn't take Einstein to figure out where that question was leading. Fuck it, I thought, why start playing games now? They would probably expect me to lie, anyway. I penciled in the block for answer B.

After the tests, they marched us to a warehouse where we stuffed duffel bags full with clothing that approximated our sizes. We went to the mess hall for chow, then were led to our barracks at the "reception center."

I lay on my bunk bed, staring at the slowly circling fan that hung from the yellowed ceiling. Torpid flies buzzed lazily in the hot Georgia evening. I rubbed my fingers along the tender skin of my scalp thinking, If the girls could see me now. I'd never realized just how bumpy the top of my head was. There's more to a man than the length of his hair, I reassured myself.

White gravy and sausage rumbled in my belly and I reflected on my dinner the day before in the cool, air-conditioned elegance of the Spanish Gardens. It would be a long time before this trainee tasted steak again.

4

Marching in Rhythm

The muffled sounds of the men around me stowing their gear in footlockers and arranging the bedding on their thin metal bunks reminds me of late fall evenings during my childhood when warm air from the furnace would rise from the register and enwrap me in a cloak of languorous well-being as I lay on my bed. The memory brings no comfort, however, for I have never felt more alone than here on this first night in the barracks at Fort McClellan, Alabama, where we have been shipped from Georgia for advanced infantry training, AIT.

I can tell by their silence that the grimness of my mood is shared by the other men in my platoon. The lighthearted repartee that marked basic-training barracks life is gone, replaced by dull stares and stiff robotic movements. The harsh realization that we are all one training cycle away from Vietnam has thrust us into a state of emotional shock.

I kneel over my boots, rubbing them with polish in an empty ritual. My heart is filled with sadness as I place my boots under my bunk and slowly unpack my duffel bag. The routine of a soldier carefully arranging his personal effects in a footlocker gradually breaks the spell of despairing self-pity into which receiving my orders for the infantry has cast me. I can hear the black soldier next to me softly humming "Michael, Row the Boat Ashore" and I quietly sing along, appreciating, for the first time, the soothing rhythm of the ancient spiritual.

The trip between the two training bases took only a few hours, but it was a journey between two worlds as different as those separated by the River

Jordan. Soon it will be time to make one more journey, and there won't be any milk and honey waiting on the other side.

Basic training was a form of mental mud wrestling in which I could never quite get a grip on the army, nor it on me. I had never been treated so rudely in my life; but once I accepted the absurdity of my predicament, I enjoyed the contest of wills provided by the military's determination to make a soldier out of me.

The first few days at the reception center were an exercise in confusion and constipation. Something about army chow got us right in the bowels. Maybe it was the saltpeter that some guys claimed they put in the food to keep our peckers soft, or perhaps it was the open-pit toilets. Regardless, our condition gave new meaning to the term *GI tract.*

Once we were assigned to training outfits, we were told that our bodies were government property. Our drill instructor informed us that we could be court-martialed for damaging them. Constipation was now a criminal offense. I gulped salt pills by the palmful, drank prodigious quantities of water, conquered my shyness, and eliminated that potential blot on my military record.

I also learned how to sleep while standing in formation. After my DI caught on, he'd slap me awake and bellow, "You're going to die, Russell. Die." It seemed like an enticing possibility those first few weeks. At least, then, I'd get to rest lying down.

We were up at 4 A.M. and out in formation fifteen minutes later, bleary eyed and bloodstained after an attack by our razors. There'd be facial hair inspection by flashlight; then we'd head out on the highway, jogging in cadence to "I Want to Be an Airborne Ranger."

The exercise did wonders for my appetite. Other guys bitched about army chow, but after two years on bachelor's rations I just slopped it on and slurped it down. Got to know grits real well. Eggs over hard. Shit on a shingle.

Easing in from our five-mile morning jog, I loved the smell of the mess hall. Gurgling vats of coffee and steaming trays of scorched scrambled eggs. Chicken gravy simmering on the gas grill. Fresh biscuits browning in the oven.

I couldn't get enough of it. I'd work my way down the serving line, scooping up as much food as I could pile on my tray, then go back for more. Ran my ass off and gained twenty pounds.

Running was a way of life. Walking was not allowed inside the company area. Whenever we were caught moving at less than a double time, it was "Hit the ground and give me twenty!" Twenty push-ups was the common penalty for all minor infractions, such as an untucked shirttail, scuffed boots, or calling a drill sergeant "sir"—a frequent mistake among overanxious trainees. The sergeant would reply, "Don't call me 'sir.' I work for a living," snap his fingers, point at the ground, and it was down for twenty.

All morning long it was hurry up and wait in the true army tradition. We ran from one class or drill to another, only to stand in formation at attention or parade rest until the DI deemed us worthy to receive instruction. It was hard to determine which they considered more important, the harassment or the teaching, but gradually we began to learn the rudiments of soldiering.

We also spent a lot of time in the low-crawl pit those first few weeks. Whenever a DI decided that our attention had begun to waver, or our responses to his commands lacked sufficient enthusiasm, into the pit we went.

Noon mess was an island calypso in an ocean of agony. The sounds were a symphony to me: the clamor of grumpy kitchen police slamming around silverware, the clanging of plates and pans, ladles and trays, the kitchen radio serenading us with "I'm a Girl Watcher" or "This Guy's in Love," and hungry trainees counting off outside the door. The out-of-shape chubby guys had to stand in a separate line, shouting out, "One fat man, Drill Sergeant," before going in for meager rations.

I'd chow down, double-time back to the barracks, and grab a couple minutes shut-eye or slip in a couple pages of *Some Call It Sleep*, a novel I'd picked up at the canteen while I was at the reception center. Then it was back out under that broiling Georgia sun to crawl some more, race around the obstacle course, or march out to the rifle range.

The black DIs called cadence. Their deep southern-preacher voices were rich with timbre and rhythm. At first we stumbled along as awkwardly as toddlers learning to walk, everybody a half step out of beat. But after a few weeks we were strutting proudly.

To march as a member of a troop was an intoxicating experience. I never felt so connected with other men as I did when our entire company stepped smartly together, the asphalt echoing with the clicking of combat boots, our arms and legs swinging in unison, metronomically, as our voices joined in song to firm bold cadences such as

Ain't no use in looking down,
ain't no discharge on the ground.
Ain't no use in going home,
Jody's got your gal and gone.

> Sound off, 1, 2,
> sound off, 3, 4.
> I don't know but I been told,
> Eskimo pussy's mighty cold.
> Sound off, 1, 2, 3, 4.

Through marching we learned to submerge our individuality into that of the group—and to someone who often had been cast in the role of outsider, it felt damn good to be part of a team.

Training magnified many small pleasures. Each drink of cool water was an experience in bliss. Ah, the sweet Georgia elixir, Fort Benning bubbly. Man-made substitutes need not apply.

Five weeks into training, our platoon sergeant called us into the dayroom for a man-to-trainee talk and a can of soda. The dayroom had a TV, pool table, and soda machine, but we'd never been allowed in there before. Nor had we been allowed to leave the company area. So, after all those weeks, this was my first encounter with a commercial beverage. The Coke tasted strangely familiar, as if it were something out of an earlier life, before I was reincarnated as a trainee. Our DI talked about poontang, penicillin, pussy, and other things, but my mind was elsewhere. All I could think of was a delicious long cool drink of water.

Oddly missing from our training environment was any sense of urgency regarding our actual reason for being there. Caught up in the frenetic daily training routine and isolated from the media as we were, Vietnam seemed to lose much of its significance. Reference to the War served as a rhetorical device used occasionally by our drill instructors as a means of gaining our attention. In terms of impact, it was greatly overmatched by the immediate proximity of the low-crawl pit.

Now and then, a Vietnam veteran would pass through the company area. We could tell he was one if he had on the uniform he had worn over there, because the insignias were muted. Instead of bright yellow stripes and badges of the sort sewed on our DIs' fatigue jackets, soldiers in Vietnam wore gray ones, for camouflage purposes. Whenever a combat vet appeared, we would stop whatever we were doing, hush up, and stare in awe. They were apparitions back from the Great Beyond. I don't believe the army wanted us to have contact with them. Too real. We might awaken from our midsummer's dream and get second thoughts about what was going on here.

George Romney had it right when he complained of being brainwashed by the military during a "fact-finding" trip to Vietnam. We were all brainwashed. The difference was that Romney was a fifty-five-year-old corporate president, an ex-governor of Michigan, and a candidate for the White House. He should have known better.

We were just a bunch of kids.

The one guy who claimed to see through all the harassment and the (to me) mindless activity that filled our days was a predental college grad named Ron Runyon. Our company always lined up alphabetically, so he and I had ample opportunity to talk. He explained the whole thing to me—the haircuts, the verbal abuse, the sleep deprivation, the emphasis on drill and uniformity. Ron said the army was trying to break down our personalities so it could remake us in the proper mold for soldiers. They were conditioning us, he said, just as a Russian scientist named Pavlov had conditioned dogs to salivate at the sound of a bell. I didn't believe a word he said. I couldn't comprehend that human beings would deliberately use psychological techniques to manipulate other human beings. I believed in personal dignity and the inviolability of the individual. After all, was I not a citizen soldier? I am in the army, but the army is not in me—that's what I told Runyon. He just smiled and offered me another cigarette.

I hadn't smoked before I was drafted, but the army gave us a five-minute cigarette break every hour. "Smoke, joke, and tell lies," the DIs said, and the pressure to conform when everyone else lit up was hard to resist, especially with Ron always passing a butt my way. I believe he was practicing a little programming on me. And it worked. He smoked Kents, a very mild cigarette. By the end of training cycle I had graduated to Marlboros.

Crude though it was, the army's technique was effective. It played to our sense of schoolboy honor. Peer pressure made this a very powerful device. None of us wanted to appear doofy in front of so many other young men.

One guy just couldn't cut it. He became known, officially, as The Doofus. Skinny and awkward, his face and body shared an unfortunate resemblance with Goofy the Dog of Walt Disney fame. He was a failure as a soldier. He couldn't march in step, chant in time, or button his fatigue jacket straight. But he was a good-natured fellow who accepted the DI's constant ridicule with fatalistic cheerfulness.

One day near the end of the cycle, The Doofus was called up on stage by our Kiplingesque company commander, who had just completed a lecture on the U.S. Code of Military Justice. With more than one hundred trainees crammed into a tiny hall, the place stank of sweat, grime, and aggravation. Mess call awaited dismissal as we sat in the smoldering heat while our lieutenant led The Doofus through a unique version of the manual of arms.

At the rifle range earlier that day, The Doofus had committed the cardinal sin of referring to his M-14 as a "gun." Now, at the lecture hall, the lieutenant ordered him to unzip his pants and pull out his penis. With one hand holding his rifle, the other his dick, the unfortunate fellow was forced to repeat after our commander, "This is my rifle, this is my gun. One is for fighting, the other for fun."

We all loved it, simply roaring with delight as The Doofus stood on stage, bewilderedly humoring the crowd. Thus ended another class on the USCMJ.

Even had we known then that the army, in its merciful wisdom, would make a clerk out of him at the end of the cycle—as it did—few of us would have traded places with The Doofus, anxious though we were to avoid an infantry assignment.

None of us draftees knew what military occupation speciality (MOS) we would be given, but we all always hoped that it'd be something other than 11b, the code for infantry. I remembered what the men back at the office had told me, how I'd probably end up in public information because of my newspaper background.

I was crazy enough to believe them.

Right up to the end of Basic it never sank through to me that I was preparing for combat. The reality of war was too removed from my experience. The absurdity of the training only reinforced my detachment. Even the live-fire exercise that climaxed our training cycle struck me more as a wild Fourth of July celebration than as Combat: Serious Business. We knew they were aiming high and that, as long as we kept our heads down, there was no danger of getting hit.

On the final day of basic training, everything changed. We lined up outside the orderly room and shuffled in while the lieutenant handed us each a mimeographed sheet with our names circled in red. I wasn't going far for AIT, just eighty miles across the state line.

My MOS: 11b10.

Read: infantry rifleman, private E-1.

Cannon fodder. Dead meat on the hoof. Grunt. Ground hugger.

So much for the cushy slot on the *Army Times*. I was running the late-sixties version of the military fast track. Five months of training, then off to Vietnam—just like Rick had warned me that crazy night in Georgia nine weeks before.

Down some dusty corridor in the dismal reaches of the Department of Payback, the formless face of the Minister of Misery must have hidden a smile. But only for a moment. As Rick said, the Minister keeps a lot of files.

It was a subdued crowd of trainees who rode that bus to Anniston. The day of decision had arrived and the army didn't waste any time loading us up and shipping us out. No time for second thoughts. During that short ride, we were in a state of disbelief so friable you could crumble it in your fingers like the red Georgia clay. None of us now had any question where we were headed next. Vietnam was no longer just a distant country where a war was being fought. It was the next bus trip, and it wasn't to Utah.

5

Riddles

The morning sun streams through the burnished oaks and russet-tipped pines, sparkling off our green helmets and the blued steel of our rifle barrels as we march down the dirt road that leads to the rifle range. Our proud voices echo off the surrounding hills as we chant, 120 voices strong:

> *When Johnny comes marching home again,*
> *hurrah, hurrah.*
> *When Johnny comes marching home again,*
> *hurrah.*
> *When Johnny comes marching home again, . . .*
> *the women will cry and the men will cheer.*
> *And we'll all be dead,*
> *by the summer of '69.*
> *The summer of '69.*

The southern tip of the Smoky Mountains looks a lot like New England. The Appalachian Trail begins nearby and goes all the way to Canada. I could hike home. It passes practically right through my backyard. They'd check the airports, the bus stations, and train depots and I'd be safe in the woods, working my way north.

Or I could stay right here. Hide in the woods and watch them march back and forth, spy on them until I understand what this all means.

My unit turns a bend in the trail, and Morse and I step off into the woods. The men behind us close the hole in the ranks and march on. The day is ours!

We are the free spirits of the company, but nobody believed we could pull this off.

We spend the day walking in the woods, delighting in our escape from the training routine. It is a reprieve we both need in order to prepare ourselves for the next stage of our lives. There is the unspoken temptation of desertion, but our hearts are not in it. Who are we to step outside our fate?

Near sundown, we return to the bend in the trail and wait for the returning line of marchers. As they pass by, we step back into formation and pick up the chant:

> *And we'll all be dead,*
> *by the summer of '69.*
> *The summer of '69.*

AIT was more than just a new improved version of Basic. A group fatalism colored our every activity. I felt like a man with terminal cancer. It was as if they had cut me open and found a Vietnam tumor inside. Inoperable, they'd said, shaking their heads. So they sewed me back up and sent me back to my unit with just a little bulge where the tumor was growing. Everyday it grew a bit larger until, finally, it would fill my entire insides. Vietnam disease, fatal every time.

As a way of treating my illness, I went on a fast. Two weeks of tea and toast and nothing more. It was a symbolic stand against training for war. A way of reclaiming my body that the army had said belonged to it. I thought maybe I'd grow weak and go crazy and the army wouldn't want me anymore. I even made an appointment with a shrink, just in case I got lucky and lost my mind.

Hell, it was worth a try, with my Vietnam tumor expanding inexorably as training marched on. Didn't work that way, though. I ran my miles and never felt tired. Did the calisthenics, hiked to the range, did it all. Combat training on no food. Felt better every day. I was still carrying that extra twenty pounds from Basic, and maybe that sustained me. But it didn't explain the great calmness that flowed through me even though I was soon to be off to war.

Near the end of my fast, we viewed an exhibition of pugil stick fighting. I sat high up in the bleachers watching two tiny men dance around, pounding at each other's bodies with long rubber-tipped poles until one collapsed and the other straddled his fallen foe, his arms uplifted in triumph.

It was hot and I was tired after a long day of training. The wind rippled the tall grass that surrounded the stadium. The smell of packed bodies, the murmur of the breeze, and the cheers of the crowd blended together in a transcendent moment during which I felt a profound sense of the interconnectedness of all things.

As we marched back to the barracks, I felt renewed, at last at peace with myself and my situation. I kept my appointment with the shrink but it was a joke. I was the sanest man alive. I had reclaimed my body, and my outlook regarding training changed considerably.

I began enjoying drill, calisthenics, and the hikes to the field. I especially appreciated weekends, when we were allowed off base on pass. A bunch of us would head into Anniston for breakfast on Sunday mornings. Grits, sausage, and eggs over easy tasted great after a week of army chow. We'd listen to romantic songs on the jukebox. I particularly enjoyed a ballad called "Can't Find the Time," a big hit right then by Orpheus, a Boston group. Most of the boys were southerners and preferred country'n'western, however. A soft-spoken fellow named Muth tried to convert me—but as much as I listened to Eddy Arnold and the like, their country twang always sounded like whining to my Massachusetts ears. I longed for the day when I could return to the land of the rock'n'roll jukebox.

Fort McClellan had the distinction of being the Women's Army Corps (WAC) basic training center. Now that we had moved into a more elevated status—AIT—we would have enjoyed the sight of raw recruits being harassed by their DIs, regardless. The fact that they were female only added to our pleasure. Their DIs were women, of course. Fierce and lean, those husky-voiced drill sergeants would bark at the girls much as our DIs had barked at us back at Fort Benning. We couldn't help but chuckle as we marched past a formation that was getting excoriated by its cadre. The southern boys would hoot and holler until one glance from the WAC DI froze the grins on their faces.

We were kept segregated from the WACs until several weeks into the cycle, at which time a social was held by the USO for all us working-class citizen soldiers. I looked forward to the event with fascination—not because I hankered for a romantic liaison, but because I couldn't comprehend why anyone, even a woman, would voluntarily join the military. Only one guy in my outfit was a volunteer, and he was a particularly immature lad who had enlisted for four years as a rifleman. We all assumed him to be somewhat crazy and felt that the recruiting officer who had signed him up should have been court-martialed for taking advantage of his naiveté.

As I danced with the WACs to the tunes of a stolid combo that sounded as if it played more at funerals than weddings, I took the opportunity to discuss the reasoning behind their enlistments with several of the young women. They all gave pretty much the same answer. They came from poor families who lived in small rural towns and had no chance of going to college or finding a meaningful career. Rather than live a lifetime of punching the cash register at the local five & dime, they had taken the army up on its offer to let them see the world. It all made sense to them, but I remained unconvinced, unable to comprehend fully why anyone would voluntarily dress in uniform, put up with constant verbal abuse, and give up total control of his or her life to do so.

Of course, the WACs did have an ace in the hole. They could always get out by getting pregnant. I didn't find any with a premature discharge on their mind that night, or any other, while I was at Fort McClellan, however. Perhaps they were saving themselves for a private first class instead of a lowly E-1 like me.

The final weeks of training were the best. We spent most of our time on bivouac, getting a taste of the real thing. We rode to the field in canvas-backed deuce-and-a-half trucks that bumped along in a way that always gave us hard-ons from the constant rubbing of our penises against our loose-fitting fatigue pants. No one wore underwear. We had learned in Basic that it quickly sweated up and ate deep creases in the soft flesh of our inner thighs.

Once out in the wooded hills, we set up camp, living in giant tents. Every meal was a picnic, to put the arrangements in the most positive light. I was chosen to spend some time training on an 81mm mortar, an infantry artillery piece that disassembled so it could be carried by soldiers and set up quickly to provide instant support in case contact was made with the enemy.

It seemed a perilous role, indeed, with all the extra weight to carry and the likelihood of being a prime target during a battle. The assignment increased my apprehension about the War. I also began to take target practice at the rifle range much more seriously than I had in Basic, though the training always held a slightly otherworldly aspect for me. Until I had been drafted, I had never used a gun. I didn't believe in killing, any more than I had believed in fighting during my school days.

Shortly after I moved to Florida, I had been challenged at the bus stop after school by the class bully, a big kid who would go on to become a noted weight lifter. He knocked me down and demanded that I get up and fight back. I refused, explaining that the whole thing seemed stupid to me.

"You mean, if I hit you, you won't hit me back?" he had exclaimed, stunned by my pacifistic response.

Once I assured him that such was indeed the case, he stomped off, satisfied that his dominance had been proven and leaving me to my shame. Or so he thought. I didn't mind. I really did think fighting was stupid. Nothing I had seen in the world since the eighth grade had changed my mind on that subject.

I also realized that enemy soldiers were not about to take the time to discuss my views with me. We would be communicating through the sight of a rifle, and I aimed to make my weapon talk straight and true. In Basic, we had trained on the M-14, a long heavy rifle with one hell of a kick. Here in AIT, getting ready for the real War, we switched to the M-16, the standard weapon in Vietnam.

The M-16s were light and short, less than three feet long, and made as much of plastic as of steel. They looked and felt like toy rifles, but we quickly learned they could be fiercesome weapons, capable of pouring out more than seven hundred rounds a minute when on full automatic. They fired so fast, in fact, that three rounds were in the barrel simultaneously and we would have to be careful not to jam the gun or exhaust our ammunition—two highly stressful situations best avoided in combat, our instructors told us.

That was a lesson I vowed to remember. The thought of running out of ammo, or holding a jammed rifle while the enemy attacked, terrified me. One thing I liked about the M-16 was that the rounds were very small—about half the size of M-14 bullets. I knew I'd be able to carry lots of them.

We also learned to aim low because bullets rise rapidly the first hundred feet before dropping later in their trajectory. With an M-16, the first fifty to one hundred feet were all that mattered, we were told. Because of its stubby barrel, it couldn't hit targets much farther away. That wouldn't matter, our instructor assured us, because most of our combat would be in close, where all that counted was firepower and the will to use it.

The issue of willingness increased in importance as the weeks rolled by. It was apparent that I was caught on an escalator—one that would carry me inevitably to Vietnam and, I was also certain, to my death.

While the thought of dying caused me to feel great melancholia, it was the possibility of being placed in a position where I would be forced to kill others that bothered me the most. I had read that a remarkably high number of American men died in combat without ever having fired their weapons. I could understand that. It's one thing to fire at pop-up targets on the rifle range, another to shoot at an actual human being, I surmised. Many soldiers, from the sounds of it, lacked the requisite fierceness to pull the trigger. And paid for it, immediately.

The day I jumped training and hid out in the woods, I did so because I needed some time off from the routine in order to think things through. I had visited a chaplain and discussed my dilemma, as I had also with the camp psychologist. Both made it clear that there was little chance of a Vietnam-bound trainee such as myself getting out of the loop this late in the cycle. CO status would have to wait until I reached Vietnam and would be even less likely to be granted once I got there.

Basically, I had two choices. I could accept the decision the army had made for me, or I could run. If I was caught, the worst they could do was put me in the infantry and send me to Vietnam. So fear of punishment wasn't an issue. Honor was.

I thought about what Muth had told me one day as we were riding the bus to Anniston on weekend pass. If we don't go, he had said, then someone else will have to go in our place. His words had spoken to something inside me that, until then, I had not fully realized existed. They touched a kind of class loyalty that I was surprised to realize I felt.

Most of the guys I was in with were from blue-collar or farm families. Their lives seemed driven by a type of peasant fatalism such as that embodied by the villagers in *War and Peace*. None had been to college, and many had not even finished high school.

The other trainees enjoyed the way I could use big words to confuse the young noncommissioned officers who formed the cadre of our training company. When the NCOs swaggered through our barracks looking for an excuse to harass us, the guys would whisper to me, "Give 'em another fifty-dollar word, Russell."

I always did my best to oblige.

Coming from the North, with my background as a newspaper reporter, I didn't fit in all that well. My fellow trainees had accepted me as one of their own, nonetheless. I couldn't deny that Muth was right. Maybe Donovan wouldn't have approved—but he could stand up on stage and sing "Universal Soldier," then go back to his estate in England. I was in the trenches with the real people and I didn't want to let them down.

The idea of combat repulsed me. I doubted that I could handle the stress and was certain I would prove to be a coward. But I decided that not to go would be an even greater act of cowardice.

When I rejoined my unit that evening I was heartened but apprehensive, expecting that I'd be punished for my dereliction. To my astonishment, no one ever said a word. I had become a military version of Ralph Ellison's Invisible Man. In the army's eyes, I was already gone. A dead man, just filling out the ranks.

Not long after bivouac, the army set us free. One month's leave and off to Vietnam. Goodbyes seemed oddly inappropriate. We sifted away like grains of sand at ebb tide, each leaving on his individual path toward our common destination.

It was probably a mistake, such a long leave. Thirty days is too much time. Time to reawaken that part of ourselves we had learned to dismiss, time to think about what our lives might have been had the War not intervened, time to reengage—however awkwardly—our civilian self.

Leave before war is the military version of a steak supper before execution. Life is prime rib, but it doesn't taste so good. I took a bus from Anniston to Birmingham and killed some time walking around the city while I awaited my next connection. After five months of immersion in army routine, I felt out of place in civilian clothes. The army had reached me at a deeper level than I realized. I was learning a hard lesson: that I could miss something I hated.

Odd as I felt, I knew I had become truly strange when my ears and eyebrows began to twitch while I stood at the bus stop. My glasses were bobbing up and down like a boat in choppy water. I buried my face in a newspaper, trying to regain control of my features. An ambulance screeched to a halt a few feet away and men in white uniforms jumped out. They raced into the restaurant behind me and, moments later, raced back out with a man on a stretcher.

It seemed an ill omen.

Welcome back to civilian life, I thought, as I boarded the bus to Tampa. I was on my way to visit my mother, but why I was going there I wasn't quite certain. It just seemed the thing to do, to touch all the old bases, south then north—sort of a farewell tour before I went to my death.

My mother and I didn't have much to discuss regarding the War. When I was a senior in high school, I had asked her whether or not she thought I should serve if called.

"It never occurred to me that a Russell would refuse to do his duty," she had replied sternly.

The subject never came up again.

Those high school days of rebellion and conflict seemed oddly irrelevant during my leave visit. My mother appeared different—fragile in a way I had never noticed before.

While I was in town, one my old friends, Michael Oreste, invited me to a Spiro Agnew rally. Agnew was Nixon's vice-presidential running mate during the 1968 election. The former Maryland governor had a reputation for baiting critics and making outrageous statements. His most memorable phrase was "nattering nabobs of negativism."

He was pretty good with the fifty-dollar words, himself.

Oreste was going with some of his New College classmates to protest the War. After Agnew began speaking, there was a pro forma draft-card burning by one of them, who was carried out by the fire marshal. Most of the other protestors left then, but four of us remained. I held a sign that read "Thou Shalt Not Kill—GOD."

Oreste's sign was equally innocuous, while one of the other two held a sign of some interest. It read "Greeks Against Agnew," and it belonged to the son of the duly elected premier of Greece, whose father had been imprisoned by the junta that had seized power there. Tarpon Springs, a Greek ethnic community north of Tampa Bay, had sent down a delegation of "Agnewettes"—high school girls in majorette outfits, who strutted their support for the ethnic candidate of their choice. Agnew was the first Greek American to run for so high an office. One of them complained about the sign, pointing out that she was Greek, and for Agnew.

The protestor discussed his father's plight with her and pointed out that Agnew was on record as supporting the junta. Then, as a genuine friend of democracy, he did the only honorable thing. He crossed out the "s" in "Greeks."

After the draft-card burning, Agnew's rhetoric got hot.

"The young people of America are spoiled," he sneered. "They flick on the light switch but can't fix the wiring. They drink water from the tap but don't know how to hook up the plumbing."

Agnew knew all about the trades, of course. As a county official, he had taken kickbacks from contractors in return for awarding government work. When this was revealed in 1973, he was forced to resign from office. Richard Nixon also had some difficulties regarding plumbers.

But Agnew was right. Many of the youth of America were spoiled during that period of unprecedented national prosperity. I, however, did not consider myself to be among that group.

After the speech, an old man attacked me as we were leaving the auditorium. He blocked my path, knocking me backward down the aisle time and again until I managed to slip past him.

"Coward. Traitor. Draft dodger," he shouted, as his shoes slammed against my shins.

I guess he hadn't done his homework.

A day or two afterward, I was on the plane to Greenfield, where I spent some time in my real home. Two weeks later, I found myself standing on a street corner in San Francisco, surrounded by a hostile crowd.

It was my last night in America. Street people, long-haired love children, gawked at the uniform I had been forced to wear to be allowed off base from the Oakland Repo Depot, a transfer station for troops shipping out to Vietnam.

The repo depot was commonly referred to as the "Oakland Meat Shipping Terminal," and I had been glad to get away for the evening. I eagerly caught a cab into 'Frisco, the Mecca of the Movement, home of the Grateful Dead and Jefferson Airplane and many other "flower power" rock'n'roll bands. Back in my sportswriter days I had always wanted to go there, but I was having second thoughts now, having become such an object of derision near the corner of Haight and Ashbury streets.

A hippie in sandals, dungarees, and an army dress-green jacket like mine stepped up close to me. His chest was streaming with medals and his hair tied with ribbons. He was much taller than I was, and bent down to be face to face.

"That's right, man, kill!" he screamed. "Blood! Kill! Blood! Kill! Blood!" he chanted over and over again, as if it were a soldier's mantra, until I broke free from the crowd and fled back to the barracks. So much for Mecca.

I spent a restless night on my cot listening to voices that swept through my thoughts with the abruptness of swallows—voices of laughter, anger, and ridicule, voices of friends and strangers, all mixing wildly together until they merged into one pounding phrase that cycled endlessly through my mind like a child's mocking refrain.

"Kill. Coward. Blood. Blood. Traitor. Killer. Blood. Blood. Kill."

Twisting in and out of my dreams, I felt trapped inside a riddle the answer to which could only be found, as in a fairy tale, in a fantasy land far across the sea.

When my plane came, I was ready to fly.

6

Mole City

A tower stands in the center of the base camp, partially hidden by a clump of trees. It flew in by Chinook helicopter this morning, dangling from a chain like a snake in the grasp of a bird.

The tower is about twenty feet high, and the land is so flat here that, with a good pair of binoculars, you can almost see Phnom Penh. From this vantage point, the defensive perimeter looks like a giant wheel with the tower at its hub. The outer rim is a trench dotted with bunkers set about fifteen or twenty feet apart. To the northwest, I can see our mortar pit. Stan and Kumo are cleaning the gun.

There are two companies in this tiny outpost in Tay Ninh Province—Bravo and Charlie, each with about a hundred men. Between us and the border there is only jungle, thick dense jungle that hides infiltration trails. Somewhere out there is the enemy—small fierce men with brown skin who have marched all the way down from the North, carrying everything they own on their backs. They have survived land mines and jet strikes, B-52 raids that blast the Ho Chi Minh Trail night and day with massive ten-thousand-pound bombs.

Now they are marching toward us, toward Mole City, where we wait, we watch, we listen. I have yet to meet the enemy, but it shouldn't be long now before we are introduced. Intelligence says they are coming very soon.

When I boarded the Vietnam-bound jet at Travis Air Force Base the morning after my confrontation with the hippies in San Francisco, I did so with an odd sense of relief. At last, after five months of training, one month's leave, and three aimless days waiting at the repo depot, I was on my way to the War.

The Braniff jet was the longest plane I'd ever seen—a stretched-out 727 that could pack in over two hundred men. I kept thinking it would never get off the ground.

But it did.

Braniff prided itself on being the hippest airline of the flower-power era. It painted its jets psychedelic reds and purples (this one had orange stripes, to boot), and its snappy TV ads featured the Air Strip, in which a sexy stewardess shed her uniform to the bump and grind of "The Stripper." Not so on this Pacific cruise. *Our* stripped-down, GIs-to-war version didn't even have headphones hooked into a music channel or an in-flight movie. After eighteen hours in which to contemplate Manifest Destiny, we stopped briefly in Guam, then made the quick hop over to Southeast Asia.

We landed in Vietnam a few days after Thanksgiving. The fully clothed, fortyish flight attendants ran a tight no-nonsense operation until we dropped down toward Ton Son Nhut Air Force Base, just outside of Saigon. Then they started gobbling over the PA system. That's right: gobbling.

I guess they had us pegged.

When I stepped off the plane, the heat hit me like a wet brick. Once inside the terminal, I was handed a leftover turkey sandwich and told to wait for a dispatch announcement. I wandered around searching for a cigarette machine carrying Winstons or Marlboros, but all I could locate was Philip Morris. Worst cigarette I ever smoked. One drag and I left the rest of the pack for the midget bellhop.

The terminal had souvenir shops that sold travel posters urging us to "See Beautiful Vietnam." One showed tourists in sunglasses viewing a firefight, in the spirit of the Washington notables who tailgated at the Battle of Bull Run, I suppose. Another poster proclaimed, "Fly United"— and pictured two geese in sexual conjugation. On the walls hung up-dated versions of the war bonds ad I had seen in the *Recorder*: grotesque velveteen drawings of tearful GIs with angelic little-boy faces standing guard in their foxholes while heinous North Vietnamese soldiers sneaked up on them with bayonets in their teeth. Underneath was written, "I spent my year in Hell—Vietnam, 1967–68." Flight jackets were for sale with this stitched on their backs: "Though I walk through the Shadow of Death, I fear no evil, for I am the meanest bastard in the Valley."

As a serviceman I'd already gotten used to the loneliness of the long-distance flyer, but this was something entirely new. There was a planeload of forlorn FNGs like me stumbling around, gawking at merchandise that seemed to commercialize our despair while short-timers DEROSing home (DEROS stood for Date of Estimated Return from Overseas, and mine was 365 long days away) shucked and jived us as if we were a bunch of honkeys in Harlem. What kind of army is this, I wondered, that mocks its own men?

Watching those guys line up for their flight home on the plane in which I had just arrived hurt so bad it just about ripped my soul in two. I felt like a prisoner in a glass cage. They looked so free, so light-hearted and optimistic, while I was trapped in trepidation and despair. All that separated us was a wall of time and, as the flight jackets so graphically stated, a one-year journey through the Valley of the Shadow of Death.

It is not often that circumstance so vividly depicts the intransigence of time and the futility of decrying one's fate. I was grateful when they called the new arrivals into formation and began processing us for our in-country assignments. Most of the guys on my flight that I knew from AIT went north to the 101st Airborne, others south with the 9th Division. For whatever reason, I ended up in the 25th, which worked III Corps, a region that ran due west of Saigon for about sixty miles until it bumped into the Cambodian border.

We rode buses with barred windows to a repo depot at Bien Hoa, cutting across the outskirts of Saigon as we did so. The streets of the capital city resembled a madman's kaleidescope, jampacked with people who rode ten deep, it seemed, on the running boards of any available vehicle while traffic flowed in several different directions simultaneously. The purpose of the window bars may have been to stop VC terrorists from tossing in grenades, as some riders speculated, or, just as likely, to prevent potential civilian passengers from throwing themselves through the glass for the sake of a ride.

I spent a night or two at Bien Hoa before shipping out to Cu Chi, home of the 25th Division HQ. There the luck of the draw landed me in Suicide Charlie, which was a long truck drive away from the cratered airstrip at Dau Tieng. The company was just getting ready to leave a patrol base near the edge of the Boi Loi Woods. I didn't know it at the time, but it would be many months before I was again in an area secure enough to drive any vehicle other than a tank or MPC (military personnel carrier).

My first morning in the field, we had a few hours to kill before hopping the choppers for our flight out to the border where we built Mole City. Francis took Pincush and me down to the barter point, where the camp followers sold soda, beer, and their bodies.

That's where I first met one of Suicide Charlie's few *living* legends, Sergeant Miller. He was toking on a cigar-sized joint and making time with the boom-boom girls. Miller looked like a *Rolling Stone* parody of *Soldier of Fortune* magazine: hair down to his shoulders, love beads hanging in loose coils around his neck, and a huge hunting knife jammed through his belt. One look made it obvious that the guy definitely was not lifer material.

He had also survived about 350 days with Suicide Charlie.

After introductions, Miller offered me a hit on his joint, but I turned it down. I wasn't about to take a chance on getting busted the first day in my new unit.

"I thought you were supposed to be a hippie," he challenged.

I shrugged off his scorn and hung tight with the other new guys, wondering how word like that had gotten around. I didn't know quite what to make of Miller. Neither did the army.

Short as he was (his time, that is), Miller should have been back in Tay Ninh City with the rest of the handful of survivors who had done their year in the 4th of the 9th's most celebrated outfit, banging hootch girls and drinking and smoking his final days to DEROS. Instead, he was shipping out with us to build a combat base right in the middle of the enemy's favorite resupply route from the Ho Chi Minh Trail into southern South Vietnam. The NVA—the North Vietnamese Army—was planning another Tet-style assault on Saigon as an inauguration present to Richard Nixon, and Suicide Charlie was one of the outfits General Creighton Abrams had chosen to break up the party. That's why the clerks back in Cu Chi hadn't been able to change my orders. The army wanted my body on the line.

Miller knew what was happening and he was enjoying every second he had left to live. He was the reason the boom-boom girls beat their breasts and wailed when we choppered out. The military, however, did not appreciate his talents to the same extent.

He'd come over to 'Nam as a shake'n'bake sergeant who had earned his stripes in a few months of NCO school rather than through years of service. Twelve months later he was still a squad leader in third platoon when he should have been a staff sergeant, at the very least. Lacked ambition, it might be said.

He'd seen a lot of gung ho guys go home in body bags, but he was the ultimate survivor. Miller had the kind of eyes that could look the Minister of Misery dead in the face and smile while calling him an asshole.

Which, I believe, is just what he called me. Then he blew some smoke in my face and wandered off into the bush hand-in-hand with a cute little mama-san.

Francis led me back to our squad's mortar pit, where Stan and Kumo were hanging loose, waiting for the 10:05 to the Cambodian border. Stan was a cocky guy with a firm jaw and thin blond hair. Kumo had softer features and a quiet demeanor. He had the dark skin of a native Hawaiian, and black piercing eyes that contrasted sharply with Stan's pale blue ones. Different though they might have been in looks, they shared a seriousness of purpose that left me wondering how they and Miller coexisted in the same outfit.

Stan quickly straightened me out on that score.

"Don't let Miller's love beads fool you," he said, after sharing a hearty laugh with Kumo once Francis told them the story of my run-in with Miller back at the barter point. "When the shit hits the fan he's the toughest SOB who ever wore an electric strawberry on his shirt sleeve."

"Electric strawberry" was the slang term for the 25th (Tropic Lightning) Division's insignia, a pineapple leaf with a lightning bolt slicing through it.

"If you'd survived as many ambushes as he has, you'd be dinky dau too," Kumo added. "He shouldn't be out here but I'm damned glad he's coming along. Miller's too crazy to die."

After they told me that, I wondered if maybe I shouldn't have taken Miller up on his offer. A chance to learn by osmosis, so to speak. There wasn't much time for second thoughts, however. A little while later I was out at the LZ—the landing zone—and loading on for my first chopper ride. It was a wild one.

We flew low to the ground so snipers wouldn't have time to take a bead on us as they would if we were high up in the air and moving slowly in relation to the surface. From my vantage point—the open door of the helicopter—everything looked miniaturized. At about two hundred feet, trees looked like shrubs and the thatched roofs of the few hootches we zoomed over looked like the conical hats the Vietnamese women had been wearing that morning at the barter point.

Sometimes, it seemed as though we dropped to ten or fifteen feet. My sense of aerial perspective was rather naive then, so we might have been much higher. On occasion, it seemed as though I could reach out and snatch a grasshopper off the bent blade of grass on which it might be sitting, but I didn't try. I had a death grip on the side of the door with one hand and a firm grasp on my rifle with the other. My feet were dangling out, and when we soared vertically—almost straight up the way only helicopters can—I could envision myself sliding out and hanging by my elbows from the sleighlike runners that gave Huey helicopters the nickname *slicks.*

When we reached our destination—a jungle clearing about the size of a small Iowa cornfield—the chopper dove straight down, then leveled off, hovering briefly at grass-top level while we tumbled out. The instant we were unloaded it split, jumping across the sky the way jets do when they kick in their afterburners.

So there we were, sitting in an empty field of elephant grass. No civilians, no houses or cars or anything with which most Americans are familiar. I could have just stepped out of H. G. Wells's time machine, or been marooned on an alien unpopulated planet. It was as if everybody's nightmare of abandonment had come true, a group vision that we had created: one hundred creatures climbing out of the primordial soup fully evolved with rucksacks, helmets, and weapons. We crabwalked to the spot where Mole City was to be sited, staying low just in case we were ambushed. But not even the enemy was there. If they had been, I'm certain they would have been as astounded by the abrupt nature of our arrival as I was.

I looked around at the grassy plain that had jungle bordering it on all sides, and kicked the dry-season hardpan with the toe of my black-leather and green-canvas jungle boot. This is it, I thought. You have arrived, Russell. I was in the War.

I was already feeling nostalgia for Dau Tieng and Cu Chi, even for Ton Son Nhut Air Force Base, but I didn't have much time for melancholia. We started digging in immediately. Harry, Kumo, and Stan were hardcore. Good leaders. Combat, for them, was serious business. They had us new guys digging and stacking and moaning and bitching all day long, and the next day too. When we weren't digging holes and filling sandbags for our own fortifications, we were doing the same for the ammo bunker and the commanding officer's HQ, or we were hauling in the heavy wooden crates of mortar rounds that a steady flow of choppers kept dropping off outside the hastily strung concertina wire, like wasps moving larvae.

I didn't know yet if I was better off in mortars than in a rifle platoon, or not. We seemed to work harder, carry heavier loads, dig more, march less, and our pay was the same. I was making about 90 bucks a month as a private first class, PFC, with an extra $67-a-month hazardous duty pay. Low wages, yes, but I wasn't in it for the money. It didn't matter, anyway. At Mole City there weren't many opportunities to spend it.

Our main form of entertainment was conversation. When you share a bunker with four or five other guys, you get to know them real fast. It's hard to remember much from those early days when everything was new. All that remain are fuzzy impressions, like a watercolor wash.

Harry, our squad leader, was an interesting fellow who seemed oddly out of place and yet fit in, anyway. He was slender, almost delicately boned, with elegant sensitive features of the sort one might associate with an actor portraying the role of an artistic youth who is studying on the Left Bank in Paris. He was also rich enough that his parents flew to Hawaii to visit him on R&R and then deducted the expense from their taxes because he was an officer in their mining firm. Why he chose to serve in Vietnam was always a mystery to me. Not many from his class did. I guess it was that Appalachian ethic of duty, honor, and country. He certainly handled command with the natural grace of a man born into authority.

Kumo was a gifted storyteller who, like any good Hawaiian, played the ukulele. In the evening, after supper, he would sit on the bunker and strum a battered instrument that he had lugged halfway around the world, banging out "Isle of Capri" while we sang along. His father had been a high school football coach in Honolulu, and his favorite stories conveyed a common theme: how the natives had knocked off haole teams in big games despite being prohibitive underdogs.

Stan walked around with the swagger of a sailor on shore leave. His brush with greatness—the date with Miss America-to-be—loomed large in his life myth. He had a quick broad smile that revealed glistening white teeth.

"You're getting the better deal," he'd tell me every morning. "I'm looking at you and you're looking at me."

He meant it.

Francis, on the other hand, came without pretensions. He was an aboriginal Bubba with a barrel chest and a pronounced drawl that was peppered with obscenities. A few of us made a bet one day as to who could get Francis to say a sentence without swearing. We all lost.

My entry was "Mary had a little lamb," which Francis transformed into "Fucking Mary had a fucking little lamb, the bitch."

Pincush made even less sense. He was short, maybe five foot six, 110 pounds, and walked with a tilt from the waist up. He also had a way of sucking water back in each time he spoke, and he hitched his pants somewhere up around his chest. If it wasn't for his Nixonian twelve o'clock shadow, Pincush would have appeared more appropriate in a thirties sailor suit—Little Rascals style—than in camouflage combat gear.

It was hard not to like Pincush, and there were few reasons to try. He blended into the group without anyone's having to make an effort to allow him to do so.

Within a few days, we felt like longtime friends, and Mole City like our lifetime home. We were well dug in. The whole idea of the thing was to dig deep—thus the name. Oddly enough, this was a newfangled idea in the 25th, if not the entire U.S. Army of Vietnam.

Our bunker was typical in that only the top two layers of sandbags rose above ground level. It connected with the mortar pit, a hole about four feet deep and fifteen feet in diameter. We also helped shovel out an extensive network of trenches that ran the entire outer perimeter, connecting each position.

Harry seemed satisfied with our fortifications—and since he came from a coal-mining background, I presumed that he had a keen appreciation of underground emplacements. For my part, I felt dumb, did what I was told, and, in general, experienced a kind of humility that had not often been mine to know.

Sometimes I thought about the enemy soldiers. I had not been fired on yet—except maybe a few stray rounds of incoming—so they weren't real. Just faceless, nameless foreboding others Out There. The rational part of my mind knew that they had bodies, names, reasons, but the rest of me understood far better the need to create apparitions. They explained so much more.

Most of the time I was too busy to think about anything other than my job. I was still mastering the basics of the mortar. It was one thing to fire rounds on the practice range back in Anniston, something else to do it in the dark without a flashlight at Mole City. Fortunately, my job as an ammo bearer mostly involved dumb work, merely keeping Stan and Kumo well supplied with mortar rounds. I needed time to make a major brain adjustment before I was ready to absorb much in the way of new information.

What little I had learned in AIT seemed irrelevant here where some sergeants had hair long enough to get expelled from my old high school and others were called by their first names. The notion of respect for hierarchy that we had been hammered with during training appeared to have lost all meaning here on the front lines. The only NCO who was held in universal respect, it seemed, was Sergeant Meredith, our platoon leader.

Sergeant Meredith was a black man with the build of an NFL defensive end and the demeanor of Rosy Grier. He was an E-7 with twenty-six years in service who'd been busted in rank stateside more than once for chickenshit infractions, but who inspired confidence in raw recruits and seasoned combat veterans alike. Sarge was a whole new experience for me—a lifer who took the time to talk to you like you were a human being. He seemed to enjoy the fact that I had been a newspaper reporter, and urged me to keep a diary so I could write a book about the War someday. Sarge's top assistant, our E-6 section sergeant, did not share the same benevolent attitude toward me, however.

Our section sergeant was a short muscular black man who derived tremendous self-satisfaction from being the only college grad in the company, other than the officers. He bragged about turning down the offer of a commission and enjoyed tossing around big words. The fact that I understood them appeared to distress him, especially after I noted his misuse of a few.

His wrestler's build—he'd been on the squad at Howard University—and cocky manner reminded many in the platoon of Bobo, the company mascot. Bobo was a chimpanzee. Whenever the section sergeant walked by, someone would mutter, "Same-same Bobo." Eventually, his nickname became simply "Same-same," which could be spoken in his presence without his understanding the reference.

"Same-same Bobo" may have been a racial slur, but that doesn't mean the men who used it were racist. They merely resented pretension and egoism and employed a convenient technique to ridicule it. Lifer attitudes met with equal disdain, as did gung ho promotion-minded commanders. For instance, the fact that we had been positioned so close to the border made Harry and Kumo suspicious about our CO, Captain Pulliman, who had arrived not long before.

They were starting to wonder how long we could go without attracting the notice of the North Vietnamese Army. Enemy units were parked just across the border, well within a day or two's march of us. I didn't like the way the veterans looked when they talked about our location—how close we were to Cambodia and how far from Tay Ninh. I was too green to appreciate fully the precariousness of our tactical situation or to realize that we had been sent here specifically to get attacked. But Harry and Kumo had Ph.Ds in sniffing out the command, and they didn't like the smell that was coming from headquarters.

"We're in some shit this time," I heard Kumo say on the afternoon of our fourth day at Mole City.

He was blasting off some marking rounds near the line of trees that sprang up only a short ways out past third platoon's section of the bunker line. Behind it lay thick jungle that would provide excellent cover for massed attackers.

"Gung-ho lifer bastards," Harry muttered in response. "One month to go, they're going to kill me yet."

"Ah, they can't kill you," said Stan, who was snapping charges.

With agile flicks of his wrist, Stan was stripping away all the little gunpowder sacks that were hooked to the tail fins of the rounds. Each sack carried a charge of black powder that would ignite when the firing pin set off the shotgun-shell-sized canister of explosive that was built into the base of the rocket-shaped projectile. The number of charges, combined with the elevation of the gun, determined how far the round would fly. In this case, it wasn't going far.

"Why's that?" asked Harry.

"Because you're too ugly," Stan answered, smiling through his gleaming choppers.

"You just wish you said that to Miss Illinois," groaned Kumo, grabbing the round from Stan's hand. "Instead of her saying it to you."

"My ass, Kumo. Hey, give me that back."

He snatched the round out of Kumo's grasp and stuffed it into my hands.

"Now, drop it down the tube, Norm," he ordered. "This end up."

I held it over the mouth of the barrel and let go, stepping away and sticking my fingers in my ears as I had learned in AIT. The seven-pound round leaped back out of the tube, whistled through the air, and came down so close that I felt the impact of the explosion and trembled at its power.

"A little taste of the poison," said Stan, enjoying my shock. "How'd you like to be on the receiving end?"

I didn't need to answer.

"Put it right on the money, eh Kumo," he added. "Right down mama's mouth."

"That's the spot," snapped Kumo.

He was right.

— 7 —

The Battle of Mole City

The message comes over the field phone.

"Get in the bunker," Harry shouts. "They're dropping it on us."

We race inside the U-shaped bunker and huddle against the front wall, where we will be protected against shrapnel. Pincush, Francis, Stan, and I crowd into the middle while Kumo and Harry guard the flanks in case North Vietnamese soldiers toss in grenades.

We are outnumbered twenty to one and our ammunition is almost all gone. The enemy has overrun Mole City, and our CO has called in artillery right on top of us. It is our only chance.

The big rounds from the huge eight-inch guns back in Tay Ninh City scream down, and the walls start rocking. Sandbags burst, showering us with dirt. The ground heaves and writhes. Instinctively, we curl up into fetal positions. Shrapnel rakes along the roof of the bunker, and in it we hear the drumbeat of Death's fingers.

Inside, the dirt is cool and moist and the air thick with our heavy breathing. Overhead, the surface of Mole City is alive with devils. Flashes of light dance along the walls of the bunker, creating ghostly images that flicker and flail as if in the throes of death, or labor.

As the bombardment continues, my terror gives way to sadness. I know I am going to die but I don't feel panic or fear, only regret that I will never see my friends in Greenfield again. They were a good bunch.

My serenity surprises me. It is that same deep calmness I felt that first night at Fort McClellan, after receiving my orders for the infantry and being transferred to AIT. Now I understand what that feeling is.

It is the calm of the dead.

Just before dusk, several riflemen from first platoon followed Sergeant José Olea as he slipped out from the base camp to set up an ambush several hundred meters to our west, nearer the border. Other groups of four men each took positions not far beyond the wire to serve as listening posts (LPs). Their job was to sit silently in the dark so they could detect any enemy troops who might be trying to sneak up on Mole City.

As I watched the hunched-over riflemen dart through an opening in the wire, I thought of fish at Halifax Gorge flitting upstream from shadow to shadow, and I was grateful to be a mortar man standing on a rock. Outside the wire, there seemed to me to be a vast wild river, one in whose swift waters I could easily drown. Inside, standing near my bunker, I felt more secure.

In a few short days, Mole City had become my home. As a child, I had always been an outsider. Being raised by a widowed mother when two-parent families were the norm may have been a factor, as was the aura of tragedy that hovered over my youth due to my father's suicide. The army changed all that. Now I was part of a community of men and glad to be in it, considering the alternative. It did not occur to me that the base camp could also be a trap.

A couple dozen mortar rounds were stacked along the wall of the parapet. I picked one up and rubbed my fingers along the slick black plastic canister that housed the round. I unscrewed the top and slid the projectile out into my hand, balancing its weight. The round felt solid, compact, deadly. The blunt nose of the brass timing device at its tip gleamed in the fading sunlight. The curved white metal that encased several pounds of high explosive (HE) tapered gracefully to a narrow cylindrical base from which several stubby stabilizer fins flared out like those on a toy spaceship. Between the fins were clips where the charges had been attached—the ones Stan had stripped off earlier during the day. With all nine charges, these rounds could fly more than five thousand meters. Charge zero would barely clear the base camp, as I had learned that afternoon. I knew why Stan had prepared them, and the thought of having to use the naked rounds terrified me.

"Won't be time to strip them down, if it comes to that," Kumo said from over my shoulder.

I slid the round back into its canister, screwed down the cap, and put it back on the stack. Stan was boiling some water on a bubblegum-sized chunk of C-4 plastic explosive, and I fixed myself a cup of instant coffee in an empty C-ration can. The thin black fluid tasted bitter, and I sipped it slowly, wishing I had some real cream to smooth it out.

While we sat around the pit, the sun dipped behind the horizon and the dark came, sweeping across the base camp like a black tide. The night deepened and the stars grew bright. I searched for constellations that I knew, but even the sky was different here, so close to the equator.

Harry returned from the command bunker, where he had gone for the evening briefing.

"The ambush has got movement," he said. "Lots of it."

Kumo slipped over to the gun.

"Think José's going to pop it?"

Harry shook his head.

"Wouldn't have a chance. CO thinks it's a reinforced regiment, two, maybe three thousand men. Told them to stay hidden. Looks like this is it, guys. A big one. Better strap up."

Harry picked up his "steel pot," which was sitting on top of the field phone, and put it on. Kumo and Stan followed suit, as did we FNGs. If imitation is the sincerest form of flattery, then Francis, Pincush, and I were models of obsequiousness that would have rivaled the courtiers to King Louis XIV. Every movement the veterans made took on weight and gravity, as ritual movements do at a funeral or a coming-of-age ceremony. On this journey into the unknown, we felt fortunate to have with us such experienced guides.

I started to cinch the strap of my steel pot tightly under my chin the way I always had before, but Kumo shook his head no and tucked the strap over the top of the rim.

"Shrapnel snap your head back," he said, tossing his own head back in description. "Maybe break your neck. Let it take the helmet. There's plenty more of those. You only got one neck. Tighten the webbing if it won't stay on."

While I covered my embarrassment by rearranging the headband in the helmet liner, I could see out of the corner of my eye that Francis and Pincush had busy fingers also. With our steel pots firmly atop our heads, we took seats on the wooden crates in which the rounds had been packed and waited while the enemy troops continued their relentless march toward our base camp.

Soon radios all along the perimeter crackled with reports from the LPs. Enemy troops everywhere. Sitting in the pit, I envisioned small men bent low, pushing through the tall grass. Dark figures silhouetted in the faint starlight creeping in from all sides, twigs and dried leaves crackling beneath their sandal-clad feet as they closed in on Mole City.

Then the radios silenced. The tiny squads of American troops were caught up in the massive flow of North Vietnamese soldiers. Trapped in a no-man's-land where they would surely be hit by both sides, they had no choice but to try to return to our base. Orders came down for everyone to hold their fire. The LPs were coming in! They hunched over, the big American men trying to look small as they joined the influx of enemy troops. Cautiously, they crept toward the wire and slipped through the gates. One man tripped a flare and threw himself to the ground, low-crawling beneath the spluttering red blaze until it burned down. Then he leaped up and dashed the last dozen or so yards to the bunker line, his comrades close behind him. Unwilling to reveal their positions yet, the enemy soldiers held their fire.

Once the LPs had raced in and scrambled into their bunkers, the night fell quiet, empty, and still. Nobody moved as we waited for the assault to begin. Pincush, Francis, and I knelt in the pit, our stomachs churning. The third platoon riflemen to our front settled over their M-16s and M-60 machine guns, grim and determined.

This was a moment for which my infantry training had never prepared me. I felt as if time were compressing, squeezing my entire life into a single instant. Everything I had ever experienced before held no meaning. I could feel my will crumbling as I tumbled into an abyss of the unknown. My past fell away and I was locked into the present, trapped in a prison of horrific anticipation from which I desperately wished to escape.

It didn't seem real, this terrible waiting. The summer of '69 was months away, and now I wondered if I'd even make it through the winter of '68. Stan and Kumo took their positions beside the gun, while Harry sat on a pile of sandbags with his hand on the field phone, waiting for the fire direction center to call in coordinates.

Somewhere out in the jungle, enemy gunners were receiving theirs, and taking aim on Mole City. Their commanders barked out the order to fire, and the assault began. Time shattered as hundreds of mortars, rockets, and rocket-propelled grenades (RPGs) arched over the wire and crashed into the base camp. There were explosions everywhere, and we raced for cover, careening into our bunker as the earth convulsed like a massive dying beast. A round hit very close by and the ground shuddered. I could hear Stan muttering, "Shit." And then, "Bastards. The whole goddamned North Vietnamese Army must be out there."

Emotions flooded through me like a stampede of wild stallions. One of them might have been fear, but I barely noticed it galloping by. I might have thought the world was about to end if it had not been for Harry and Kumo sitting quietly with their legs folded against their chests and their eyes half closed, calmly waiting out the incoming. My mind went blank, and eternity passed; then the earth stopped trembling. The barrage had finally lifted.

"Let's move!" Harry shouted, and we dashed back out to the gun, Stan and Kumo in the lead. There was a brief eerie silence, as if the air itself were holding its breath. Harry grabbed the field phone, waiting for firing instructions. Kumo bent over the gun, and Stan grabbed a round. Francis, Pincush, and I crouched at the parapet wall, unsure what to do. Then the ground assault began.

Squads of sappers threw themselves at the wire, exploding shape charges to blow holes in the concertina. Hundreds of enemy troops rushed in close behind them, opening up all at once with their AK-47s. Instinctively, we ammo bearers reached for our rifles as the men on the bunker line returned fire. I crouched low, transfixed by terror, as bullets screamed overhead and green tracers slashed across the sky. Harry called out firing coordinates and Stan and Kumo went to work, firing rapidly, aiming for the staging areas out in the trees where legions of NVA troops waited, ready to charge the base once our bunker line had been breached by the assault forces. Our gun gulped down the rounds stored in the pit, and Harry shouted for resupply. Francis, Pincush, and I began dashing from the pit to the ammo bunker and back with more mortar rounds.

Swarms of enemy troops hurled themselves at the third platoon bunker line directly in front of our position. The American soldiers knocked back the first assault, firing furiously. Enemy bodies lay strewn across the ground, some dead, the wounded still firing. The second wave attacked. NVA soldiers slithered across the death zone, using the bodies of their fallen comrades for cover, creeping in closer and closer, heaving grenades at the firing ports of our bunkers. The next wave, behind the second, poured in a murderous fusillade that overwhelmed our fire. One bunker fell silent; then another. The NVA troops climbed over the top and dropped into them, their bayonets ready. They slashed into the wounded Americans, ripping apart their bodies, then slid into the trench and moved down the line.

As the bunkers fell, one by one, more enemy troops surged toward third platoon's side of the perimeter, knocking out the remaining positions until only Sergeant Miller's was left. But he was not planning on dying. Fighting alongside the platoon sergeant, he was manning an M-60 as well as an M-79 grenade launcher—just belching fire. He was determined that no NVA soldiers were going to claim his love beads for a war trophy.

We ammo bearers were totally defenseless as we raced for more rounds. Fire was pouring in on us, and Miller was providing our only cover. We'd streak for the ammo bunker, which was about fifty feet away to our rear, grab three rounds, and charge back. When we reached the pit, we dove straight in, bullets screaming over our heads.

It was then that I learned that the infantryman's best friend is not his rifle; it's a hole in the ground. Anytime, anyplace. If they had slopped that pit full of ooze and slime and diced in a few bloodsucking leeches, I would have dived right in like any soldier worth his combat infantryman's badge (CIB), happier than a pig in shit. I guess that's why they called us "grunts" and "ground huggers."

The hardest part was climbing back out again.

It wasn't courage that inspired us to make that mad dash time and again. It was simple desperation. Stan was dropping rounds as fast as we could carry them back. Fighting was intense all along the perimeter, with more bunkers falling to the enemy and our entire base camp threatened. The CO kept radioing Tay Ninh for more artillery, but Command wasn't responding. Our little 81s were plugging the gap where third platoon used to be, and our supply of ammo was dwindling fast.

A couple Phantom jets swooped in close just outside the perimeter, dropping napalm bombs that exploded with an incredible sonic blast as the flame sucked in air to feed the inferno. Two, three, four times, I counted, as they dove down on their raid. I knew I should be grateful to the pilots, but all I felt was resentment. They were up in the air while I was trapped on the ground. I never wished to be someplace else more in my life than I wished to be in the cockpit of one of those Phantoms as they roared over the base camp heading back east to Tay Ninh. At that moment, I understood the eternal enmity between the pharaohs and the boulder pushers. It hardly seemed fair that they could just fly away while we had to remain behind.

Despite the air strikes, our situation worsened. Once the enemy command realized that they had knocked out third platoon, they moved in for the kill. Hundreds of troops streamed out of the woods to our front, and there was little to stop them but our three guns. Harry shouted for Kumo to try to break up the assault by firing the charge zeros. Stan started dropping the prestripped rounds down the barrel while Francis ripped bare some more. The ammo bunker was almost empty, and Pincush and I cleaned out the rest. We were down to white phosphorus, and—Geneva Convention be damned—we stopped the charge briefly with a furious barrage. But there seemed an endless supply of reinforcements, and they kept charging the bunker line, inspirited by the anticipation of triumph and certain that our base camp belonged to them.

It almost did.

In a final desperate act, our CO called for the artillery rounds—which had started to arrive, all right, too little and too late to prevent the catastrophe—to drop right on top of our position. At first the artillery squadrons back in Tay Ninh balked, but the captain pleaded with them that we were on the verge of extermination. The rounds were vertically timed devices (VTs), set to explode just before impact so they were not likely to blow up our bunkers, but certain to kill anyone who was out in the open. Harry got the word, and we fled into our bunker.

Hours had passed since first we had huddled in there waiting out that initial barrage, but it felt like seconds. I was still locked into that moment, imprisoned inside a bubble of time that expanded endlessly. Nobody spoke. We pressed our backs against the inside wall, anticipating a direct hit from one of the mighty eight-inchers or else a grenade tossed in by an enemy soldier who was desperate for cover and wanted to take our place.

The explosions were enormous. It didn't seem possible that our bunker could stand up to the blasts. I remembered reading about the "Lonesome End," Bob Carpenter, the West Point footballer who had been written up as a hero for calling artillery on top of his position after being overrun, and I figured I had reached the end of the line myself. Once I accepted the inevitability of my death, I moved beyond terror. Somehow my life no longer seemed so important. I didn't see God, or experience a brilliant flash of illumination. I just felt calm and very very sad. What saddened me the most was that I would never see my friends again, the friends with whom I had so much fun the year before.

After all those years of poverty and depression, living in the shadow of my dead father, those times with them were the first really good times I had ever had. For that one brief period, the shadow his death had cast over my life had lifted, and now it was over. I was going to meet my Dad.

So I waited, quietly accepting the fate that I had anticipated ever since receiving my induction notice. It's hard to know just how long the six of us shared that silent communion with Death. It could have been a few minutes; it could have been hours. In a sense, it never ended.

After a while, the pounding stopped. The artillery barrage had stopped and, miraculously, we were still alive! Uncertain what sort of reception to expect, we gripped our rifles and crept outside, ready for one final bitter act of combat.

To our front, Miller was still blowing smoke, holding down some NVA troops who were trapped in the trench line. For the most part, the base camp was quiet. The bodies of enemy soldiers lay sprawled across the ground like so many twigs tossed down by a fierce storm. We crawled from the pit and worked our way around the immediate area, checking for live bodies, but we didn't find any. Among the enemy dead we found some Americans, as well.

Just off to our rear, the bunker of a "triple-duece" mortar squad had taken a direct hit, and all six guys were laid out cold, never to warm up again. Several of the guys who manned perimeter bunkers that were open at the back side where they faced into the base camp had been hit by shrapnel from the VTs, it appeared. A few may have died from it.

Others had obviously been shot during the battle. It is the third platoon lieutenant that I best remember. Young, tall, rigid as an oak branch, he lay sprawled face forward in the dirt, a hole in his back the size of my fist, and his mouth frozen open in a perpetual soundless scream. As we carried his body over to the chopper pad, I could almost hear him talking to me. Let me out of here, he was saying. I want to go home.

Or maybe that was me talking to me.

Sergeant Olea made it back in after trading grenades with the NVA throughout the night. But three of his guys didn't, and seven others left on a medi-vac chopper. Only some excellently controlled artillery fire that surrounded his ambush with a cocoon of steel kept his group alive after they were spotted by the NVA.

While we cleaned up the rest of the bodies, some guys with a 90mm recoilless rifle took target practice blowing out a few bunkers crowded with NVA soldiers who woke up too late for the morning bus back to Cambodia. After that, I leaned against my bunker, bit my lips, and wiped a few tears from the sides of my eyes. I choked back my sobs because it didn't seem soldierly to cry.

As the sun rose over Mole City, I could almost feel my soul harden. Something deep inside me shut down. If the boy I had been the day before still existed, he was buried beneath an avalanche of horror as real as the dirt that would cover these dead soldiers' graves. If I had looked in a mirror, I would have seen a stranger staring back at me.

Could this have really happened? I thought. For an instant, an odd sense of detachment overcame me, as if I could be anyplace I chose to be. Then I remembered the jets that had flashed through the night, leaving me behind, and I realized that I was very very tired. It had been a long night, and the adrenaline was all gone. I needed to get some rest. It was morning now—but it would be evening before long.

In the nights that followed, I learned more of what terror is. One simple sentence tells it all: Are they coming again tonight? For eleven more months I would ask myself that question almost every single night. Usually they did not come. But there were times when they did.

The dark always came. And I guess it always will.

8

Routine Shit and Santa Claus

Shit-burning detail, right around Christmas. Me and a couple guys from Bravo Company meet up at the latrine area, wheel out the converted oil drums, and start roasting maggots.

It takes a lot of gas, a lot of stirring, to burn fifty-five gallons of shit. All I can think is that there must be a curse upon the land. It's 100 degrees in the shade and I am out in the hot sun stirring gurgling vats of human waste like some kind of goddamned Shit Wizard conjuring up the ultimate evil spell.

One of my detail buddies says to me, "At least now, if you meet a Vietnam vet when you get back to the world and he says he's seen some shit you'll know he ain't lying, brother."

Talk about getting literal.

I pour some gasoline from an olive-drab jerry can while they vigorously stir the thick fetid solution. We all step back and I toss in a match. Flames shoot up toward the broiling sun. We stir and pour, and stir some more, until all that remains in the oil barrels is a dusty pile of carbon. Then we put the drums back under the brace of wooden-frame toilet seats. Detail done, I ask the Spec 4 in charge if I can return to my squad.

"Sure thing," he answers. "But first tell me, man, what's your sign?"

I shrug—astrology's not my bag—and his buddy answers for me.

"He was born under the shit star, on the cusp of crap."

Cooked bodies do strange things. Rip open, split at the seams, detach at the joints. Sorenson—another new guy assigned to second squad—and I were leaving behind a trail of human debris as we hauled NVA bodies to a mass grave outside the wire.

A few days earlier, someone in our outfit had tried to burn the bodies. He had soaked them with gasoline and flicked his Bic. Human beings are 78 percent water, so all the corpses did was blacken on the outside and boil within. The result was chicken-fried humans that came apart easily.

Sorenson and I developed a system for moving the bodies, but it didn't always work. As I pried up one leg with a rake handle, he would loop a rope around the ankle. Then we'd both pull. If we met a little resistance, or the body was particularly well done, the joint would disintegrate and we'd be left dragging just the foot. Sometimes, when a body arched over a hump in the earth, the belly would split open and the bowels spill out. Occasionally a head rolled off, for no apparent reason, as if the neck were a rotted piece of string. So we were moving bits and pieces, all the way to the grave.

After dirt was pushed over the mass grave by a bulldozer flown out specifically for that job, I went back to my parapet for a dinner of C-ration spaghetti and meatballs. A chopper from Division HQ circled overhead, broadcasting tinny carols and canned seasons greetings from our commander.

It was Christmas Week 1968. I had pulled the dead-man detail after losing a bet to Francis. He went to see Bob Hope back in Cu Chi. They took one front-line soldier from each squad and sat them all in the front rows. The rest of the place was filled with REMs, such as the guys who had ridiculed me when I was first assigned to Charlie Company. Francis filled us in on the show when he got back. He especially enjoyed the scantily clad starlets Hope paraded on stage between one-liners about military life. Francis had a good time—but I didn't mind. I never cared much for Bob Hope's brand of humor.

We'd all shared a good laugh a few days earlier after an upside-down mortar incident from which I earned the nickname "Ab," as in Abnormal Norman. The night of the incident we had heard the by then all too familiar oomph, oomph, oomph that meant incoming, get to the gun, now! It was pitch dark, the middle of the night, when I jumped up from my bedroll to race out to the gun, and I ran the wrong way, slamming straight into the rear wall of the bunker. Dazed, I staggered out to the pit.

Harry had gone home, and I was now the assistant gunner. My job was to drop the rounds down the tube. Pincush handed me one and I grabbed it by the fins, lowering it down the barrel nose first.

Everybody froze, terrified. If I let go, the round would have slid down the tube, and the detonator at its tip would hit the firing pin. No one knew what would happen next. It might explode, or it might not, but nobody was curious to find out. I hung onto the round, dimly aware that something was wrong. Stan leaped over, wrapped his hands around mine, and yanked the round back out. Pincush took over my job until I got my bearings back. By then everybody thought the incident was pretty funny, and in the morning we posed for a group picture, reenacting the scene.

That was about it for holiday excitement, though we did have several unusual visitors. High-ranking ones, the type who usually didn't come any closer to a combat patrol base than we did to the air-conditioned dinner clubs in downtown Saigon. Before they arrived, word came down to clean up the base camp and smash all clumps of dirt down to the size of a quarter—no small task at Mole City.

A lot of very important people wanted to check us out, and it wouldn't do for them to stub their toes. We were about to become a Must See on the Vietnam Tour. Admirals, four-star generals, perhaps the very people who sent us there to get killed, were coming to gawk at us and marvel at the fact that we were still alive. The irony of the situation was obvious. I wouldn't have minded their dropping in for the day, if only they'd stayed the night.

Francis was in his glory, swinging an eight-pound sledge, whistling Sam Cooke's "Working on the Chain Gang" with the soulful angst of a stripes-clad bad ol' boy doing time on the county line. He was being backed by a chorus of grumbling grunts as the heavy weapons platoon pounded away with shovels and pickaxes.

We were still mourning the loss of nearly forty men, and nobody cared much for the chickenshit lifer Mickey Mouse crap. As a life experience, this one ranked somewhere between shit burning and opening a can of C-ration ham and eggs, the eating of which was out of the question.

In the spirit of a guy who had worn a Pinellas High T-shirt to class to protest segregation at Largo High, I set about redressing the situation. For once, my years in Florida paid off. The number-one tourist trap in Indian Rocks Beach had been a place called Tiki Gardens, which boasted models of the giant stone Tiki gods of Aku-Aku on Easter Island. I'd also seen pictures of Stonehenge, a (some said) magical circle of rocks built by the ancients in England. The miracle of cultural cross-pollination inspired me with a vision of "Clodhenge."

I collected the largest chunks of hardpan I could handle, and dragged them over by my pit. It was no small effort. Some were at least four feet tall and two feet in diameter. I arranged them in a rough circle that approximated the points on a compass. Then I stood back and dusted my hands. It was a nice piece of work.

Initially, Sarge did not agree. Now, I'd quickly learned to love that man. We'd often sat out in the evening shade and talked about lifers, uniforms, and all that kind of stuff. I was certain that he wasn't the guy responsible for me pulling dead-body and shit-burning detail. Same-same Bobo was behind that, for sure.

I'd made the tactical blunder of telling Same-same that I didn't believe any man had the right to tell another what to do—words that quickly found Sarge's ear and may have cost me some early opportunities for promotion. But Same-same didn't know shit from a salami and I didn't care what he thought. Sergeant Meredith was a different matter entirely. He was a great man—one of the best I'd ever known. I always figured that, if we ever got overrun again and had to flee out into the jungle, he was the one man I'd want to stick close to. If anyone could bring us back alive to Tay Ninh, he was my pick. I would have run through walls for the guy, walked across hot burning coals barefoot, or jumped into a freezing river naked, if he asked me to.

But that doesn't mean I was above trying to make a fool out of him.

I presented Sarge with the persuasive argument that not only was Clodhenge a piece of art that represented the Spirit of Mole City, but it also served a utilitarian function as a massive direction-finding device. In the smoke and chaos of battle, I told him, people get confused. They lose their sense of direction, both figuratively and in actuality. A quick look at Clodhenge would straighten them out and renew their fighting spirit. Each of the four major points of the compass was marked by a mighty Clod God. For the lesser declinations, Lesser Gods of varying heights marked the spots. And if we did get overrun again, what better site to rally defenders, with cover on every side and the Mole City Spirit to look over us all.

Sarge bought the argument, or at least enjoyed the absurdity of it, and soon I was proudly explaining the meaning and purpose of Clodhenge to my CO. Captain Pulliman seemed to have a taste for twisted logic—how else to explain his decision to assume command of Suicide Charlie—and he went along with the goof. A little while later, our local "light bird" (slang for lieutenant colonel) swooped down for a gander. The battalion commander had earned the undying enmity of Charlie Company's troopers by choppering out of Mole City minutes before the big attack. He figured to be a sucker for my rap and, sure enough, he swallowed the whole thing in one big gulp. Next I knew, admirals and generals and their coterie of courtiers were dancing their clumsy cotillion among the Gods. Clodhenge had made the map.

I was one swelled dude. It was the proudest moment of my military career—with the exception of my discharge, of course, and the time I failed to salute a four-star general.

Eventually, however, the act wore thin and the iron law of uniformity won out. Sarge sent Francis over to pulverize the Gods, which he happily did, ruthlessly wielding the hammer of Thor. Perhaps he was envious of all the attention I had received. But I knew—and, more importantly, they knew—who had got the best of that one.

So we battled on, the army and I, in the real war of the Draftees vs. the Mindbenders. The winner of that one is a little hard to call. The Minister has it in his files, no doubt. He keeps all the records. I told Stan about the Minister, and he said that if I made it home, then, sometime when the moon was full and I'd drunk about a quart of bourbon, I should go out and ask the Minister who won.

We talked about a lot of things those long hot days after the battle of Mole City. The CO kept us mortar guys close to our guns while the rifle platoons swept the area on a daily basis. The captain had lost faith in Division Artillery after the battle, fearing that they would fail to fire if one of our patrols ran into some shit. By keeping the sweeps within five clicks (each click being a thousand meters) of our patrol base, they were always within range of our mortars, and the CO knew he could count on us for instant accurate support.

Waiting at the gun made for a long day, however, and I frequently wished I could be out with the riflemen, hiking through the countryside. Sarge promised that this would soon be the case, once they had pacified the immediate area and began traveling in a wider arc. Then we'd be lugging the gun or, preferably, filling in a few of the holes in third platoon. Until then, we had to find creative ways to pass the hours.

War is one of life's most boring activities, most of the time. Our main release from tedium was cardplaying. Rook was the game of choice my first couple months in the platoon. The dry season in Vietnam means a near cloudless sky every day, with no relief from the scorching hot sun. At midday we would descend into a bunker—usually the one built by Phil and Erik, the FDC guys—for a few hands.

The fire direction center (FDC) group represented the heavy weapons' brain trust. Inside that bunker during the bedlam of a fight, Phil, Erik, and Same-same too, I suppose, engaged in the mysterious computations that transformed map coordinates into calibrations for the sight on our gun. In a pinch, we could fire free-form, aiming visually at the target and walking the rounds in on it. The way this was done was by bracketing, firing short, then long, and splitting the difference until—bamoo!—HE on the hot spot. Most of the time, however, targets weren't in the line of sight; when they were, distances could be deceiving. When firing near our own troops, as was sometimes the case, we didn't want to be dropping in any short rounds.

Phil and Erik were our best and brightest. Phil had grown up in Nepal, the son of missionaries, and was very comfortable in a Third World environment. He had also been chosen Trainee of the Cycle back in his Basic days, despite not having a lifer bone in his body. In many ways, he complemented Francis, being a direct opposite. He never swore, was not often heard to complain, and once, when we happened to be in Tay Ninh together and near a piano, I said how about a quick performance of Beethoven's "Moonlight Sonata." Without hesitation or a score, he hopped onto the stool and knocked off a tough but sensitive interpretation of that famous piece. Buck Owens's "Tiger by the Tail" was not in his repertoire.

Erik was a curly redhead, as his name might imply, with large brown freckles that splotched up most of his tall skinny body. He did everything with an attitude of exactness that brought comfort and good vibes to the guys in the line platoons who depended greatly on the quality of his calculations. It was he who kept the cards. Rook requires a special deck, no face cards, but is otherwise much like canasta, pinochle, or whist, with bidding and trump suits. Growing up in the country in a big, poor family meant lots of hours at the card table, so our Mole City rook sessions, for me, were a bit like a return to childhood.

Occasionally we discussed childhood themes while we played. One day the subject switched from the usual topic, what we would do when we got back home, to a new one, what was the most disillusioning moment in our lives. I don't know who brought it up—probably Phil, who had a penchant for philosophic discourse. Anticipating profound and moving commentary on the absurdity of war, of friends dying for no good reason while protestors were storming the gates of Washington, I was amazed to learn that, to a man, all present but me shared the same faith-shattering moment: the day they found out there was no Santa Claus.

I guess I had missed something along the way. I couldn't remember ever believing there was one.

In the depths of the FDC bunker it was always cool compared to our dusty pits, and Erik and Phil—being the well-put-together troopers that they were—always managed to hang onto their mosquito nettings, as well.

As the winter progressed and rain became more frequent, insects began to become a bit of a problem. They buried their eggs in the dirt, where we lived. And whenever the occasional downpour struck, the larvae would hatch in droves, all with the same kamikaze spirit, their only wish a taste of GI blood before they died. Mine seemed particularly appetizing. Some nights the air literally roared like an urban highway with the giant proboscis-wielding pests. The first response on the part of us FNGs was to shower down with insect repellent. The vets told us we'd regret it, that the army's lotion would burn our skin until it was raw with sores—and they were right. "Live and let live" was the motto when it came to Vietnam's remarkable world of insects, but that approach didn't help me one night when I got bit by a centipede. We measured Vietnam centipedes in inches, not those tiny European delineations; and this one must have been several inches long. Anyway, I was tossing and turning in the throes of dementia, so Kumo sent me to the aid station for assistance. The corpsman stuck a thermometer in my mouth, and a few minutes later I heard him whisper, "104," to his buddy. Shortly thereafter, he reappeared with a needle about the length of a small dagger and nearly as thick. Fortunately, my ears were still working well enough that I also overheard the same fellow say to his partner, "Let me give it. I've never done a shot before."

One look at that needle and I made it clear that the *experienced* medic would be doing the plunging, or forget it.

I can't remember if the medic had to brace his foot against my buttocks to pull the needle back out or not; but when that double shot of penicillin and streptomycin hit my system, I darn near passed out. It worked, though. Next day I felt fine. Maybe it was fear that cured me, not the medicine. Fear that, if I went back for more, the other guy would demand his turn.

Eventually we became so grimy that our own smell must have kept the bugs away. A sudden cloudburst was our only chance for a shower. When it rained in Tay Ninh Province, it really rained. There was no halfway about it. One moment, not a cloud in the sky; the next, dense torrents teeming down; and the next, clear as a bell again. We'd race out into one of those mini-monsoons, strip down and lather up fast, praying it would last long enough for a thorough rinse.

Later, when the rainy season arrived, showers were no problem at all. But January was a dry dusty month, which was just as well. Mole City, after all, was almost entirely below ground. On the few occasions when the heavens did open up, our trench line became a spillway of swill, and the bunkers all had indoor swimming pools.

After shit-burning detail, a shower in swamp water would have been a welcome relief, but I usually had to settle for a warm can of soda instead. Much to my dismay, I became a bit of a regular at the sweet slop shop. Eventually I started to suspect that Same-same might not be responsible for these choice assignments. It occurred to me that perhaps Sarge was letting me in on a secret army code of behavior in his oh so subtle way. Rule number one: Wise guys burn shit.

I don't believe there was a rule number two.

9

Team Sports

Shortly before sundown, Kumo flicks on the radio. His favorite show is about to air: Compulsion, *an old-time radio thriller about people driven by madness to commit horrible crimes. In the end, like the fellow in Poe's famous story "The Telltale Heart," it's the character's very fear of revelation that leads to his or her demise.*

We cluster about the small portable, Stan, Kumo, Mike, Francis, and I rimming the pit, while a breathless penitent recants his crime, much to Kumo's delight.

Tonight's sinner had worried so much about his wife's possible loss of affection for him that he drove her away by his jealousy, then killed her out of anger when she took up with another man.

"Ain't that just like a haole woman, huh Stan," *he says, as the credits fade from the air.* "They got you coming, they got you going. Guy can't win for losing."

"Sure thing," *Stan replies, giving me one of those broad winks that crinkle one side of his face.* "Not like those native girls. All they want to do is wiggle their hips inside those grass skirts and do the Big Island hop."

"Aw, shit," *says Francis.* "Would you guys stop talking that way. Like to give me a fucking hard-on."

"Wouldn't know what to do with it if you had one," *Pincush interjects.*

"Why you fucking little pencil chewer, I sure would," *Francis replies.* "Ain't but one or two women in all of LaBelle would tell you otherwise."

Francis is excited, and the way his eyes bulge when he talks makes us all laugh; but beneath the rough humor is an undercurrent of tension. We are all

young men who have not had sex for a long time, and it's painful even to dis-
cuss the subject. Kumo pushes the antenna down and puts the radio in the
bunker for safekeeping.

"Better give Bobo a visit," he tells Francis when he comes back out. "Bobo
will show you what to do."

We all know what he's talking about. When our mascot gets bored, he hops
up and down and plays with himself. The chimpanzee has no qualms about
public ejaculations.

My favorite time of day at Mole City was early evening. Right after supper, with the line platoons back in from sweep and the enemy mortar
squads still rubbing sleep from their eyes, we weren't needed at our
guns. Surfeited with excess energy after a day of waiting near the pit, we
mortar guys would set up a volleyball net and take on our counterparts
in Bravo Company.

Kumo and Stan were excellent players, as were Phil and Erik and several other guys. According to Kumo, Suicide Charlie had placed second
in the Ton Son Nhut Air Force Base volleyball tournament the previous
summer when our unit was stationed closer to Saigon. He claimed we
would have won it, in fact, but the judges were all air force guys so they
cheated to ensure victory for their own.

Regardless, we always did a number on Bravo. Feelings of resentment
still ran high because there was a perception that our sister company had
failed to defend adequately its half of the perimeter the night of the
ground assault. Kumo had lost some friends that night, and he wasn't
about to let Bravo forget it. We played jungle rules. A typical spike involved grabbing the net with one hand and yanking it down low, then
coming down with a fist to the ball—and if a defender was parked underneath, so much the better. The games never broke up into fistfights,
but there were a lot of black eyes and bloody noses. The fact that Bravo
Company tolerated this sort of behavior on our part did imply a lack of
guts on their part.

Another favorite activity was football. There was a grassy area on the
Bravo side of Mole City large enough for a truncated gridiron. Sunday
mornings there was no sweep—the search-and-destroy missions during
which the rifle platoons went out looking for enemy munitions caches.
Some men chose to attend church services; others got together for a
game of two-hand touch.

Our best player, by far, was a fellow named Rocko, a second platoon
90mm recoilless rifle operator who had played defensive end at Slippery
Rock State College during its twenty-seven-game undefeated streak, the

longest in the nation during the mid-sixties. Rocko was a solid six foot four and had an arm like a slingshot. Like most defensive players, he harbored a repressed desire to play quarterback, and in our game he played whatever position he wanted to. The football was not as rough as the volleyball, perhaps because the potential for serious injury would have been so much greater, but the field conditions did add a few interesting hazards. There were bunkers and mortar pits to leap over or around and, even more treacherous, numerous craters left over from the barrage of incoming the night of the ground assault.

Wide receiver had always been my best position in high school, and racing under Rocko's rainbow spirals provided me with great joy. He could toss the ball almost from one side of the perimeter to the other. I've always felt that the greatest catch I ever made on any field was one at Mole City, when Rocko lofted the ball into the stratosphere as I hurdled across pockmarked terrain in my combat boots. Feeling a bit like Willy Mays in the 1954 World Series when he made his great over-the-shoulder catch on a Vic Wertz drive to deep center, I looked up in time to reach out for the ball while in full stride. As my fingers wrapped around the pigskin, my front foot entered free-fall. My concentration on the catch was such that I had stepped into a deep crater without realizing it. I went down like I'd been shot and was dazed by the impact, but I held the ball and that was all that counted.

Athletics had always been a passion of mine, and it was great to be able to compete even in so remote a spot as Mole City. As a former sportswriter, I was also happy to indulge my vocational interests by listening to the Armed Forces Radio Network (AFRN). Life in a different time zone offered the advantage of real-time broadcasts of major sports events at odd hours of the day, and we had lots of odd hours.

The main sports activity back in the States that January seemed to be plane hijacking. For one streak shortly after New Year's Day, planes were redirected to Havana or Tripoli twelve or thirteen days in a row. We followed the radio news reports with captivated interest, wondering when the first GI on his way to 'Nam would get the clever idea of switching destinations. Either none tried or that was one report that didn't make it past the censor's desk.

If Americans named years the way they do in Oriental countries, 1969 would have been called The Year of the Underdog. Not only did "Those Amazing Mets" win the pennant, but those amazing Jets won the Superbowl. Perhaps it was The Year of New York City, as well.

My one full summer at the *Recorder*, 1967, had been highlighted by the year of the Impossible Dream, when the Boston Red Sox, a.k.a. the

"Cardiac Kids," became one of the few teams ever to go from worst to first. The Sox won the American League Championship on the last day of the season when Jim Longborg beat Dean Chance, a twenty-game winner, for the second-place Minnesota Twins, in the showdown for the gonfalon, as we sports scribes like to call the pennant. I'd followed the Sox from a distance during the summer of 1968—about one thousand miles distance, at Basic—but my heart wasn't in baseball like it had been the summer before. Football was another matter.

The American Football League had a team in Boston—the Patriots—but I hadn't paid much attention to it when I was sportswriting. They'd sent me some press credentials, but I tossed them under the table and forgot about them. Like most New Englanders, I was born to be a Giants fan, but I gradually developed an interest in the AFL, if only as a concept. They were the upstarts, the underdogs whom the establishment NFL mossbacks constantly ridiculed. Once I was in the service, I found it easier to identify with the new league and regretted my earlier dismissive arrogance. In a very real sense, the AFL captured the spirit of the times. Improvisational, a bit ragged around the edges but full of vitality, they represented rebellion, new ideas, the hope of change. They also landed a TV contract, and the quality of their play started to improve more quickly than the senior league realized.

Early one morning I caught the 1969 Superbowl—Jets against the Colts—on AFRN. That was the game when Joe Willie Namath promised victory for the upstart AFL and delivered, mainly on the strength of a rock-ribbed defense and the educated toe of field goal specialist Jim Turner. With those 4-F knees, Namath always had trouble getting the ball into the end zone; but Turner kept popping the pigskin through the uprights, and the Colts were held to one touchdown. I'll always remember that last drive. The Jets got the ball deep in their own territory and crammed it down the Colts' throat behind the powerful rushes of fullback Matt Snell. Ran the clock out, the way a champion is supposed to.

Joe Willie got all the credit, of course. That's how the system works. Same way the army awarded decorations. The day our medals came through for the battle of Mole City, several of us in mortars received Army Commendation Medals for Valor. We had a rollicking good time reading the boilerplate write-ups aloud to each other. They began: "With total disregard for his personal safety . . ." You fill in the rest. Won the war single-handedly, caught bullets in his bare teeth, stuff like that. Hyperbole, thy name is Army.

The officers got silver stars, naturally. They probably deserved them, though I wouldn't be surprised if our chickenshit battalion commander picked up a DSC for flying the friendly skies.

One guy who did get what he deserved was Sergeant Miller. I heard him on the radio a couple weeks after he went home a certified hero, one shiny silver star tucked in his breast pocket.

"I sure as hell wasn't going to let them kill me," Miller told the interviewer. "I only had ten days to go. I was too short to die."

It felt good to hear his voice. Just to know that he DEROSed made one sense that all was not wrong with the world. Vince Lombardi was eating crow for claiming that the AFL was a league of wimps, and Sergeant Miller was smoking hootch with some blond-haired blue-eyed American mama-san.

Sort of in his honor, I tried a taste of the local weed. Teamed up with Phil—of all people—to cop a jay and smoke a number. Didn't do much for me except rocket me to the top of Sarge's shit list, if I wasn't there already.

Somehow or other, he found out about our little excursion into cannabis madness. Phil told me later Sarge didn't say much about it. Just said, "You did something you shouldn't have done," to his prize trooper and let the matter drop after Phil promised not to go astray again.

He didn't say anything to me. That was the unnerving part. I guess he decided I wasn't worth bothering with or, more likely, he was too busy dealing with all the personnel changes caused by the one-year rotation system the army maintained during the War.

Our squad picked up two new members sometime in late January or early February. The first was a guy named Lucky, who had tattoos of dice on his arms, talked with a gangster accent, and looked about forty-five years old. What he was doing in the infantry was somewhat unclear. He seemed a character straight out of a World War II movie who belonged in the boiler room of a ship steaming for the South Pacific. As his nickname implied, he talked a lot about big-time gambling, though Yahtsee was about the heaviest he got into it with us. He liked to talk to the dice when he shook the cup, but the results never indicated that they were paying much attention.

The other fellow was a baby-face guy named Melvin, who came from somewhere in the Upper Midwest. Melvin had quite a roll of baby fat that, combined with his buck teeth and freckles, gave the impression of an oversized twelve year old. Despite appearances, Melvin was actually a much better soldier than Lucky, who had a tendency to disappear when duty called, while Melvin threw himself right into the task at hand, no matter how undesirable the activity might be.

Lucky didn't stick around too long, though I'm not sure where he went or when he left. In the field, equipment had a way of just disappearing. You started out with a full complement of gear: rubber pancho, pancho liner, field jacket, wool blanket, all the extras. After a few months all that remained were the essentials: rifle, bullets, something to wrap up in during a cold rain, canteen, and bayonet. People were the same way. Some just kind of wandered off when you weren't noticing. They got reassigned, I suppose, for mysterious reasons only the army fathomed. But it did make sense that Lucky left and Melvin stayed, so perhaps it was the hidden hand of Sergeant Meredith at work once again.

Vietnam has been described as a one-year war fought ten times, due to that replacement policy. Just about the time a guy really knew what he was doing, he became a short-timer with only one thought on his mind: to keep as low a profile as possible so he could get back to the Real World safely. As a result, the most dangerous parts of a soldier's tour were the first three months, when inexperience could get him killed, and the last three months, when his mind had started to wander to the green fields of home.

In a sense, the War was also a different one for every man who served. It all depended on where and when he was there. I couldn't have asked for a worse assignment than the Manchus. We were a bastard battalion attached to the 25th. As a result, Division Command considered us ultra-expendable. Another bastard unit—the Wolfhounds—shared our fate, oftentimes rotating positions with us. During the Korean War, the Wolfhounds became famous for initiating the last bayonet charge in the annals of the U.S. Army.

Tradition didn't mean much to me, but it was big for the army. Wherever the shit was thickest, there we were sent. The army has an odd way of rewarding success. The better the job a unit does, the more action it sees. Combat is one of those activities that must be learned through experience, and Suicide Charlie had lots of experience. If we, or the Wolfhounds, weren't available, then Command sent in a 1st Air Cavalry Battalion that also operated out of Tay Ninh. Apparently it was still being punished for losing its colors in Korea. The Minister of Misery never forgets.

Some spots in-country were definitely much safer than others. During the year I was there—late 1968 through 1969—Tay Ninh Province was the hottest spot in the War.

Major General Ellis W. Williamson had taken over the 25th Division about the same time I was in AIT, and he had decided to change the way the War was being prosecuted. His idea was to turn the construction of patrol bases into offensive operations through the "Force Fed Fire Support" system, in which patrol bases were built close to a suspected NVA line of march, basically inviting them to hit it. Williamson also altered the shape of the patrol bases, from ellipses to circles, and had them built smaller so they could be manned by one or two line companies. Gambling that the NVA would only hit one base at a time, he could then concentrate all his firepower in the one battle and blast the NVA with it.

Mole City had been the first test of his tactics, and it had apparently been successful enough, in his eyes, that he decided to try it again. It was the Wolfhounds who took the second shot. They built a place called Diamond I, about two clicks from the border, and on February 23 the NVA took them up on their invitation to the big game. Just like at Mole City, the enemy soldiers broke through and it took ten hours to drive them off.

We heard stories of the Diamond disaster secondhand, so I don't know just how many guys they lost—but it wasn't enough to discourage Williamson. He had them build a couple more Diamonds, and he had further plans for Suicide Charlie, as well.

As a result, War Zone III—where the 25th Division operated—had the highest percentage of American KIAs in Vietnam, and the most contacts with the enemy during the winter/spring of 1969. Nobody in Suicide Charlie would argue with those numbers, though things did quiet down considerably after we'd staked our claim to a couple acres of Cao Dai country that night of the long knives in late December.

The NVA had taken terrible losses during the battle—several hundred men from one of its finest regiments, if you could believe Command. As a result, the North Vietnamese soldiers gave Mole City a wide berth as they infiltrated toward Saigon. That meant we had to go out and find them.

10

The Sweep

It is late afternoon as we reach our destination, a field of high grass where choppers will lift us back to Mole City. Sweaty, tired, we move quickly past the few stands of trees that dot the open terrain here on the Cambodian border, our thoughts centered on showers and supper.

Inside a clump of bushes, a man and a boy tremble, waiting for us to pass, knowing that the slightest movement or sound could betray them. They stand still as statues as more than one hundred men of Charlie Company hurry past. Beside them sit a 60mm mortar and several high-explosive rounds.

Pincush and I are pulling rear security. After humping nearly twenty clicks, we are both beat, and I walk right past the bushes without noticing the people hiding inside. It is Pincush, with his accountant's eye for detail, who spots the movement.

"Someone's in there," he says, and I walk over. Melvin, too, and the lifer E-7 who fought beside Miller in third platoon's last bunker. He nods yes to our unspoken question and we open fire. Here on the border, nobody is an innocent.

We pull back as the rest of the company, startled by the gunfire as if slapped awake from a deep dreamless sleep, doubles back to see what's happened. The man and the boy crawl from the bushes.

As they stagger out, dazed and bleeding, I take cover behind a giant anthill that towers over the grass like an insect highrise. The man holds up his arms in surrender but the boy falls into the dirt, too weak to stand. Moaning, he crawls toward me.

"Shoot him! Shoot him! He's got a grenade," shout the men in my company as they close in around us.

I motion for the boy to stand, or at least to put up his hands, and he struggles to rise. Our eyes lock together. I feel a spark pass between us as if our souls are embracing. Urgently, I signal for him to get up, but he collapses again as the bloodcry intensifies.

"Don't shoot. He's wounded," I shout back, but nobody wants to hear me. They are angry, frightened, impatient with hate.

I know I should run up to the boy and help him, but I don't dare, unwilling to risk my own life to save his. His eyes are pleading, begging me to rescue him, but still I hesitate.

The noose of men draws tighter around the boy, their weapons locked and loaded. A medic runs up, drops into the dirt beside him, and rolls him over to treat his wounds.

The boy has no grenade.

By the time March rolled around, life at the base camp had become a very dull scene. The morning chopper from Tay Ninh would bring in thermos cans of coffee, eggs, and grits and we'd eat breakfast at the new mess area, then stroll back to the pit and clean the gun. We restocked ammo, policed the area, and did the slowhand shuffle until mail call. Rook had fallen out of favor, so we'd play a few hands of euchre with the Indiana farm boys who hadn't made it into the national guard. When the mail arrived, I'd read my daily letter from Kelly, who'd rediscovered the writing habit once I got overseas, and count the minutes until lunch.

The afternoons were equally exciting, minus the distraction of mail call. Though I was in the infantry, I wasn't getting much exercise and I was restricted to an area not much larger than the topside of an aircraft carrier most of the time. My sorties into the countryside were restricted to a few jogs outside the wire to guard the barter point.

My first time there, I struck up an acquaintance with two small boys who had brought with them a rat in a cage. It seemed an odd pet so I asked them why they had brought it along.

"Eek, eek," one said, imitating a squeaking rodent. "Chop-chop."

He smiled and rubbed his belly.

Between the sign language and the pidgin English, his meaning was clear, but I was still a bit taken aback later in the afternoon when they yanked the rat out, killed and dressed it, and roasted it over a spit. One look at that and I handed right over the can of C-rats peaches I'd squirreled away for an end-of-the-day treat.

The barter point at Mole City was short on action. Perhaps it was the proximity to the border, or perhaps the Vietnamese who lived in that area had too much self-respect to spend their time servicing American GIs. Ice was also in short supply this far from Tay Ninh, which took some of the fizz out of the beer and soda market.

Eventually, Command decided that the area around Mole City was officially pacified, and the opportunity came to start going out on sweep. I jumped at every chance I got.

Some days we filled in holes in the line platoons; some days we lugged the gun. As assistant gunner, my job was to carry the barrel while Stan handled the tripod and Kumo the sight. Pincush was responsible for the base plate and the other guys, Francis and Melvin, carried two or three rounds. It was no small task, humping all that hardware in addition to our M-16s and enough ammo to give them some purpose.

We must have presented a ridiculous sight, staggering along those rice paddies trying to keep our balance under all that weight. We never got ambushed, though, and I'm sure the reason was that the enemy soldiers were laughing so damn hard they couldn't find their triggers.

After that horrific night of the ground assault, the absurd side of the War did seem to manifest itself a bit as winter rolled into spring and the uneventful became commonplace. A year is a long time to a twenty year old, and time now seemed a greater enemy than the Enemy as the memory of the terror receded a bit from my consciousness. The nightly harassment of incoming mortar and rocket rounds had also lost its impact, reduced to a mere annoyance rating somewhere between army chow and tropical insects on the Irritability Index.

Combat duty, I was starting to think, was an extended version of that training dictum: hurry up and wait. I guess that's part of what those first three months in-country were all about, picking up the rhythm and learning to adapt to the sporadic quality of contact without losing the edge you need when the shit hits.

One day in early March, as I was reaching the end of what might be called my apprenticeship period, I went out on sweep with Pincush and Melvin, filling in some slots in rear security. Sleepy, but apprehensive, we walked the dawn trail out of Mole City, instant coffee and reconstituted eggs jouncing in our stomachs as we passed through the wire in a long thin line and entered that other world Jim Morrison and the Doors sang about. We were strangers in a desperate land, walking the Cong's highway.

The regular riflemen tended to look on us mortar guys with disdain. But I figured, to hell with them, I'd earned my CIB, too—and if I had to be an infantryman, I wanted to get into it. I had bandoliers of ammo strapped across my chest Pancho Villa style, a pack of Pall Malls stuck in the band of my camouflage helmet cover, grenades flopping from my utility belt, and my automatic rifle tucked against my rib cage with my finger on the trigger. I was wearing faded fatigues, and my boots had never seen polish. I weren't no FNG no more. I was one tough-looking son of a bitch. A Manchu Motherfucker, the meanest bastards in the Valley. It was said that we had a price on our heads of fifty dollars each, greenbacks. And if that was so, then we were paying it back in lead. We were walking zombies from the Dawn of the Dead.

I didn't mind being at the back of the file. I liked the feel of the rear. It was the closest thing to that day in AIT when I wandered off with Morse. I wasn't planning on doing any solo hiking in Tay Ninh Province, but I dug the illusion of solitude walking at end of the file provided. I still thought I could take the Army, the War, and Vietnam all on my own terms.

As a result, I really enjoyed the forays into the countryside. If the Lord ever made a prettier place than Vietnam, I've never been there. No smog, no factories, no honking horns and traffic jams. Not where we were, anyway. As we humped along in the morning breeze, the tall grass glittered with dew. In the distance I could see a small settlement, a communal well surrounded by thatch huts. It was just like a scene from a children's picture book. I smiled as I remembered the lines: "I can run, I can run, fast as I can. You can't catch me, I'm the Gingerbread Man."

A little further on we passed our usual jumping-off point: a hootch with a hole in its roof that had never been repaired. We'd found an old man in there the day after the attack. Died with a hard-on. Supposedly, he'd been warned to clear out, but he was a stubborn old fellow and he stayed put. Artillery round found him before we did.

Usually, we split to one side or the other at the hootch to start a giant loop that eventually would bring us back around to Mole City. But this time, after tightroping some rice paddies that patchworked the area, we headed due west, straight for the border. I guess the CO must have been getting bored with the local area, or maybe he had some inside information about where the NVA had stashed some munitions. Some days we'd seem to have a plan—spots on a map where intelligence suggested food or equipment might be cached. Other days it was just catch as catch can.

Command made a big deal about locating enemy supplies. The Powers That Were seemed to think that uncovering enough rotting rice and rusty rounds would grind the mighty North Vietnamese War Machine to a halt. Fat chance. Robert McNamara, Mr. Number Cruncher himself, supposedly gave up on the War when he became convinced the North Vietnamese could conceive babies, raise, train, and arm them faster than we could kill them. The same held true for supplies. We were bombing the hell out of the Ho Chi Minh Trail with Operation Arc Light and similar bombing campaigns, but it didn't make any difference. Air wars probably never do, in areas that are all mountains and jungle. Stopping enemy infiltration was like trying to stop the rain. It would have taken a solid line of soldiers stretched from one end of the country to the other, and even then they would have figured out how to get through. By 1968 there was enough stuff buried in Tay Ninh Province for the NVA to fight twenty more years without resupply. Cu Chi was even worse. There were so many tunnels under the city that more people could fit beneath it than above. As a result, little guys became tunnel rats; their job was to go down under and ferret out the enemy, armed only with a .45 and a flashlight. It took a special breed to do that duty. Fortunately, I am not small.

The closer we got to the border, the quieter it became. I guess any civilization has a hum to it, even the low-tech kind. I noticed that the riflemen seemed a bit tighter than usual, quieter as well. I also noticed that it was getting very hot. After three months I'd adjusted fairly well to the temperature, which averaged nearly 100° F. during the day and in the high 80°s at night, but it was obvious this day had record-setting potential from the way my body was sloshing around inside my uniform. The captain was really moving us, too, seriously covering some ground, so that by noon we'd already done ten clicks—nearly a typical day's humping. About then we stopped for lunch near an abandoned homestead. Surface well, a couple blown-out hootches, and a small stand of palms that swayed in a light breeze. We spread out in a long semicircle, straddled our steel pots, and popped open some C-rations. They might be leftover from Korea, but after half a day's march they tasted damn good.

I sat down next to Mike Pincush and tore into my double ration of spaghetti and meatballs. One thing about going on sweep, it always made me hungry. I was down to 145 pounds and still shrinking. Thin men make smaller targets, which was good. Too thin, though, and it's down in the tunnel you go.

We didn't talk much—just dug the cool breeze, sucked in the clean country air, and mellowed into the break. It was hard not to lay back and relax. I didn't feel much like a target right then.

"Gonna' be a scorcher," said Mike, draining his canteen. "I haven't been this hot since yesterday. Where are the soda boys when you really need one?"

Mike was right. The soda boys who sometimes followed us when we went on sweep, hoping to make a few bucks off thirsty GIs during lunch break, were nowhere to be seen. They kept their distance this close to the border. Troopers tended to get a little trigger happy here in no-man's-land. Apparently, it was all free-fire zone at this intersection of map coordinates.

Villagers were expected to know better than to wander too close to an American unit on the prowl. Not many people lived out here, and those who did were mostly Cao Dai, a staunchly anticommunist religious sect that had the third eye as its holy symbol and was founded just after World War I by a mystic who held a strong affinity for the eclectic. The Cao Dais recognized the divinity of Christ, Buddha, Victor Hugo, Sun Yat-sen, Joan of Arc, and—one suspected, after dealing with the soda boys—Adam Smith. I was told they had a temple with wax effigies of the above in Tay Ninh, but I never saw it. They also had previously had their own army, which once fought the Viet Minh in the streets of Saigon. Their anticommunist credentials were longstanding.

As a result, we didn't deal with the Viet Cong much. Our enemy wore gray uniforms instead of black pajamas. At least, so we thought. But we could never really know where anyone's sympathies lay unless they were pointing a gun at our head. Even the soda boys' loyalties were questionable. Sometimes they knew a whole lot more than they let on.

"Hey, look at that," Mike said, grabbing my arm and pointing at the abandoned well where a couple of new guys had fixed up a rope and bucket system using belts and a steel pot and were drawing up water. They knew enough not to drink it—probably poisoned—but they were pouring it over their backs, and it did look like fun. I stood up, thinking to join in, but Pincush pulled me back.

"Don't do it, Norm," he cautioned. "If I was a gook with a gun I'd shoot them first. Kind of piss you off, don't you think?"

He had a point. Not wishing to suffer the potential wrath of the Guardian of the Well, or whatever spirit it was that those fellows were defaming, I checked my enthusiasm. Anyway, we were supposed to be keeping a lookout. A surprise attack right then could have been an out-and-out massacre, but the possibility seemed unlikely. The hard thing to understand about Vietnam was that the place was so tranquil most of the time. It looked like a fairy-tale land. Even the people made sense there, tiny, with soft childlike features and tittering bird-song voices. If it wasn't for the bomb craters everywhere and the hardware I was packing, I could have been back in time a thousand years. In a word, Paradise. Of course, "Paradise" is the Arabic word for where fighters go who die in the Holy War.

Vietnam was a paradise where one carefree step could be your last, where, hidden in a clump of bushes or crouched behind a rice-paddy dike, a group of men could be waiting with only one thought in mind: to shoot you dead.

Talk about a bad attitude.

The order came to saddle up, and we packed our trash, cutting the empty cans at both ends and crumpling them underfoot. No need to leave extra paraphernalia for booby traps. Taking one last drag on my Pall Mall, I crushed that underfoot as well, grinding it into the dirt, then field-stripping it for good measure. No enemy trooper was going to smoke my butt.

Overhead, a "freedom bird" twinkled in the brilliant sunshine. My heart soared with it. The three months since I'd climbed onto that Braniff jet at the Oakland Repo Depot had been the longest days I had ever known. Vietnam gave new meaning to the expression *one day at a time.*

I settled into my twenty-click gait. My shoulders were hunched beneath the weight of my pack as my eyes followed the vapor trail of the jet plane. Sadly, I watched the firm white smoke diffuse into the blue and vanish, not a trace left behind.

I was thinking "Leaving on a Jet Plane," the Peter, Paul & Mary classic, and dreaming the dream of the late rising sun. Pincush poked me with the tip of his gun barrel.

"Wake up, Norm. You're in Vietnam, remember?"

I turned and nodded.

"Looks more like the Midwest to me," I replied. Then, remembering the crazy saxophone player who gave me a ride to Florida. "Or Utah."

We both laughed. It didn't matter where we were. What counted was time. And we were doing the hard kind.

It would have been cooler in a bunker back at Mole City, but I was glad I wasn't there. We passed through a field that was blooming in yellow flowers and I picked one, tucking it through the lapel buttonhole in my fatigue jacket. In case of an ambush that flower was not real smart, but I was in a romantic mood, willing to believe that kindred spirits in the NVA would be less apt to shoot a guy with a corsage.

As the afternoon rolled on, it got hotter and hotter and that flower wilted until it was just a damp splotch with a golden hue. It was humid, I was sticky, and my postlunch glow faded. The weight of a thousand wrongs pulled me down. There was nothing I would have preferred more than to strip off my sweat-soaked fatigue jacket and dive into a cool mountain stream. Massachusetts boys like me just weren't made for that kind of heat, but I couldn't help notice that our Chieu Hoi scout still had on his field jacket and hadn't even broken into a sweat.

Chieu Hois were cold-blooded guys, renegade enemy soldiers who switched sides for twenty acres and a water buffalo. Nobody was quite certain whose side they were on, but ours hadn't betrayed us yet and he knew the terrain like a native. If he did know where the enemy was located and deliberately led us away from them, not everybody in our unit would have been disappointed, nor those on the other side.

We passed into a thickly forested triple-canopy jungle region where it was so dark we almost had to knot trunks to tails to stay in a line. I don't know if we were looking for somebody—a lost enemy unit perhaps—that might wander out there perpetually sort of like the Ancient Mariner, becalmed in the jungle trees, or if we were just practicing night march during the daytime. Whatever the purpose, we followed a trail, so the going wasn't as slow as it would have been had we needed to chop through with machetes. Nonetheless it was still late in the day when we popped out on the other side. Whatever it was that we were searching for, we had not found.

The thought of a cool refreshing ride back to Mole City and evening chow became increasingly more inviting as we made our way through the last few stands of trees and hurried to an open field of elephant grass for a rendezvous with a flight of choppers the CO was ordering up on his radio. The captain walked past the bushes where the man and the boy were hiding, just like all one hundred of the other guys. I did, too, until Pincush caught that glint of movement out of the corner of his eye and called us back.

The lifer E-7 who was pulling rear security with us was a skinny fellow with the kind of leathery skin that looked as if it had been stretched across a rack. It was bronzed so deeply that it shone. He had blue eyes and pencil-line lips that dipped down instead of up when he smiled. Like most men his age who were still in the infantry, he had a quizzical air about him, as if he were perpetually inquiring of fate how it was that he had ended up in this war, at this time, in this place. Undoubtedly, his night in the bunker with Miller at Mole City had increased his curiosity. Anyone who has seen much action knows that the possibilities of surviving combat are quite limited and decrease proportionately with each encounter with the enemy. As a middle-aged man in a young man's uniform, he was certainly aware that caution was more important than compassion. He had no fear of firing and didn't consider long before nodding in affirmative to Mike's question.

I had a brief war of wills with myself before tugging on the trigger of my M-16, resisting, at first, as Melvin and Mike punched off a few rounds. It seemed odd firing at something, someone, I couldn't see; and I was reluctant to let those bullets go. It hardly seemed necessary. Whoever was in there was certainly outnumbered.

The rattle of our M-16s brought the rest of the company back in a flash. By then, we had stepped away several paces and our victims were crawling out toward us. The cries of the riflemen to shoot them made no sense to me. It seemed both cruel and unnecessary. I couldn't see taking a chance on being eradicated by a fanatic, but it was obvious these two people were seriously wounded and that blasting them again would only satisfy some primitive desire for vengeance. Or maybe it was fear that drove the other men to scream for their heads. Regardless, their survival was in immediate jeopardy. I motioned for them to raise their hands in the universal gesture of surrender, while maintaining my spot behind an ant mound that provided at least the illusion of cover. The older guy did just that, but the young one could only toss his arms up and collapse in the dirt. The longer he remained prostrate, the louder and more insistent became the cries to shoot him, and I waited anxiously for him to respond.

When he did, he raised his head up and looked into my eyes with a plea of such desperation that my heart broke. All of his sadness, his terror, and his uncomprehending agony passed onto me—his legacy to the brutality of war.

I was riveted by fear, shame, paralyzed by my inadequacy to redeem the situation. For all I could tell, the boy might have been a teenager, but he looked eight or nine. He survived the wrath of my comrades only because one of our medics ran to his assistance. Doc, as we all called him, was a black man and the bravest man in our company. He was a conscientious objector who frequently walked point even though he didn't carry a weapon. To call him "fearless" would belittle his character. I'm sure he experienced fear just as great as the rest of us. But he had a purpose in this War—one that I did not share. He didn't care which side of the wire you were on: If you'd been hit, he would wrap your wounds.

Doc pulled that boy back together and cinched him tight to a stretcher to be medi-vacced out. I was dimly aware that something terrible had happened. I had made eye contact with the enemy, and now they, he, had become real. The only reassuring aspect to the situation was that, thanks to Doc, it looked as if the boy was going to live. While he and the man were taken back to Tay Ninh for treatment and interrogation, we caught our flight to Mole City, relieved but shaken. Supposedly, the two had a mortar hidden there in the bushes with them and, if Pincush hadn't spotted them, we would have been chopped to pieces at the LZ.

We showered, ate our chow, listened to late-night Radio Vietnam, kept watch during the dark hours. The next day we went back out on sweep, we mortar men being now respected all the more by our CO for helping prevent a possible massacre, but sweep was never the same for me. I had always thought of the enemy as a man like myself, not as a child. Watching that boy twist in pain there on the ground had left me very angry, but it was not an anger that was easily defined. I was furious at the enemy for putting a child in a position where he could get so terribly wounded, and I was equally upset with the men in my own unit who wanted to shoot him when he was down. Unlike Mole City, where the NVA was clearly the aggressor, this time ambivalence abounded and there was no clear villain on whom to pin my rage.

I thought about the boy a lot as the days and weeks passed, as I crossed out the numbers on my short-timer's calendar or sat at the bunker, staring out into the night. I thought about how he had pleaded with his eyes, how our souls had met and touched, how that spark of awareness had passed between us. I thought about it all quite often, and sometimes—when the days were dark and the nights darker, when Vietnam seemed interminable, a year that stretched into decades, a series of lifetimes passing, one atop another, all in the space of days and weeks—I thought about how little it mattered that I could not help him when he needed me most. Not because of Doc, a good man with the courage to do the right thing. No, not because of him. It was something else, the words of a guy from my company who came in from Tay Ninh a couple days later. Concerned, I asked him how the boy was doing.

"What boy?" he asked. Then, remembering: "Oh, him. Never made it in. They threw him off the chopper to make the old guy talk."

11

Enemies

"I don't want to go to war. I don't want to leave my fiancée, my studies, my family.

Last night I pedaled the streets of Hanoi. They city felt so dark and empty. Dark in case the bombers came. It made me sad to know that I would never walk down by the river with my fellow medical students again. Never again sit by the water and hold hands with Kim.

No one ever comes back. My neighbors, my uncle, my father. All gone. Dead? We don't know. No letters. No messages. We never hear from them.

Never.

(A month later.)

My foot is terribly sore. Infected. The soles of my sandals are worn through. Two days ago I stepped on a jagged piece of metal that made a deep cut in my foot. I try not to say anything, the other men would think that I am weak. The pain is almost unbearable.

(Two weeks later.)

We have crossed into the South. All day we hide in bunkers forty feet underground, waiting for the B-52s to pass over. The earth shakes as if we were inside a volcano.

Sometimes, we get caught in the open. Slowly, my comrades are disappearing. The Uncle Soldiers search for us all the time.

Our leader says that soon we will reach Saigon. I am ready. Yesterday, we were spotted in a field during daylight. An FO called in artillery, and many, many comrades died. We are few who remain from those who started the journey. Only just a few. Soon, we will be none. Soon, we reach Saigon.

I am happy. I feel blessed. When we attack Saigon, many Americans will be killed.

I just want to kill one Uncle Soldier before I die."

—*Diary of a North Vietnamese soldier*
(*printed in the 25th Division* Tropic Lightning *magazine*)

A couple hours after I was told that the boy had been tossed off the helicopter, I started vomiting. It was evening and I was sitting at the pit drinking a cold can of Pepsi. Somehow, we had scored a thermos can with ice—a real find—and Stan and I were sitting right on top of it.

For whatever reason, our mortar platoon had been relocated to the opposite side of Mole City, the area once occupied by Bravo. It was our third or fourth move since we'd landed there the past December. Why they kept shifting us around was a mystery to me, and probably to them as well. One more move and we would have made it all the way around the clock.

That Pepsi was tasting mighty good when I was struck by an irresistible urge to regurgitate. I made it out of the pit and off into the bushes before I lost dinner. I didn't find it again for over two days. After a while, all that remained to come up was a thin white spittle, but every thirty minutes or so my stomach would tighten and, fight against it though I did, I would retch like a man who had too much to drink.

Eventually even I realized that something was seriously wrong, and I went in search of medical assistance. One of the improvements that had come to Mole City was the installation of a battalion aid station now manned by a middle-aged major instead of just the corpsmen who had shot me up in January after the insect bite. There I received some muscle relaxants to stop the spasms and a white substance to coat the lining of my stomach. They did an excellent job of curing the symptoms of my disease, but the cause could not be determined by the doctor.

He was a surgeon with a full kind face and a gift for laying on hands, which I learned when he massaged my stomach before prescribing a remedy. As he talked about the perils of army chow, hot weather, and strange microbes that lived in tropical climes, his soft fingers searched out my pain and set it to rest. By the following morning, my stomach felt good as new and I was back in the mess line ladling on the sausage and white gravy.

Though I quickly regained my appetite, my enthusiasm for sweep took longer to recover. Given the choice, I stayed back on the gun. If we had to hump that sucker, fifteen pounds of base plate got heavy in a hurry. I usually started out with it tied across the top of my rucksack. By noon I would be wearing twin grooves in my neck and shoulders. After a while, I became very adept at balancing it on top of my head, and I would carry it there, looking more like a peasant woman lugging water than a combat infantryman.

On days like that, I really earned my pay—all $140 a month of it. But it was the nights that we were really hired for. While we didn't have to go outside the wire for ambush and listening-post duty, that didn't mean we got to sleep straight through, either. We stood shifts, two hours on, two hours off, all night long, alternately manning the radio or pulling bunker guard.

Long nights, little sleep, that's the way the War was. Sleep deprivation was a fundamental biological state for all of us. My ability to seem awake while somnolent caused me some trouble one night when a squad mate woke me for my radio watch shift, then headed off to his bunk roll. Apparently I talked with him a bit and convinced him I was awake. Truth of the matter was, however, that I was sound asleep and never did get up and go over to the FDC bunker. As a result, the radio went unattended the rest of the night. Fortunately, no one needed mortar support that night, but I got a grilling in the morning once the dereliction was discovered.

I imagine the upside-down mortar incident lent credibility to my protestations of innocence, and a new rule was instituted: that your replacement had to be up and walking, not just prone and talking, before you could consider yourself relieved.

One device installed purely to annoy us was the firing of harassment and interdiction rounds, which we called H&I. We'd align the gun before dark, then stagger out for random firings during the wee hours. What impact this sort of activity had on the enemy was impossible to measure—none at all, is the most likely finding—but engaging in it certainly interdicted our sleep and left us feeling quite harassed.

The enemy engaged in a similar sort of practice, of course, but they had one distinct advantage: they knew where we were. Ground assaults might have lost their attractiveness, but harassing us with mortar and rocket fire provided them with ample opportunity to relieve their insomnia.

The night former President Dwight D. Eisenhower died—March 28—I was pulling bunker guard duty and listening to the radio. I was staring out into the darkness, counting bushes, when they interrupted the standard programming for the special announcement. No mention was made of his warning to Lyndon Johnson about the foolhardiness of becoming involved in a land war in Asia.

As if to commemorate his passing, the enemy blasted a few rockets our way. I dove into the trench as one flashed straight at me. It exploded with such light and fury that I was sure I was a goner—that it had hit the bunker beside me and I was about to be perforated like an IBM punch card.

Actually, the hit was close, but not that close. The rocket had passed overhead, then smashed into a bunker about thirty feet to my rear where three men were sleeping. Such is the odd nature of explosions, however, that the men went totally untouched. The power of the impact was so great that most of the shrapnel blew straight on through and out the other side. The only man who was wounded was a fellow from my platoon named Schell who had been sitting on a parapet wall about twenty yards away and hadn't gotten flat enough. He took some shrapnel in the chest—not serious—and one of the medics dug it out while the rest of us returned to our guard posts, a bit more alert than we had been five minutes before.

The rocket attack was typical of what we were putting up with at the time. In a sense, we were dealing with two enemies at once. By day, we searched for the NVA regulars. At night, our main concern was Viet Cong guerrillas. The VC were the more notorious of the two. They were called "Charlie" by American troops, or "Sir Charles," after an ambush. VC weren't too numerous in our region, we believed (and as the relative absence of booby traps suggested), but they could be anyone from a child wrapped in explosives to the commander of the local Popular Forces outfit. There was no certain way of knowing. Sometimes Charlie was even the camp barber.

When a Vietnamese barber gave a haircut, he didn't stop with the scalp. He would shave our eyebrows, the short white hairs on our foreheads and upper backs, all with a long straight blade that could have slashed a throat as easily as it did the fine strands of our postadolescence peach fuzz.

The morning after the attack on Mole City, we found our barber dead in the wire. He'd been in the day before, no doubt on an intelligence-gathering mission; and a few guys had taken the opportunity for a quick shearing. Stan was one of them.

"How he must have wanted to slit my throat with that straight blade of his," Stan speculated later. "'So sorry, GI,' he'd chirp, as blood gurgled down my white cloak. Then he'd smile apologetically and move on to the next guy."

We were cutting each other's hair for a while after that, or waiting until those rare opportunities when we found ourselves back in Tay Ninh for an afternoon. By late March it had become clear to our CO that his unit wouldn't be seeing civilization for some time yet, so he instituted what he called "one day stand-downs."

Each platoon would take turns sending a guy in for a day so he could shower, get a haircut, maybe see a movie or go to the post exchange (PX) and buy new batteries for his radio. There were also massage parlors in Tay Ninh, where a fellow could get rubbed down all over, so to speak.

Tay Ninh was a pretty safe spot. The city itself had a population of over half a million, and the adjacent base camp held several battalions. The permanent party lived in wooden structures there—no bunkers for *them*, unless the place was under direct attack, which was known to happen now and again. The airstrip was a favorite target for enemy gunners, but perhaps the most devastating blow ever delivered at Tay Ninh was in the mess hall. Workers there most have been VC, and one day they snuck in enough explosives to blow the cafeteria sky high, taking out about twenty guys who should have ordered lunch to go.

Some areas, such as the Mekong Delta and the Michelin rubber plantations near Dau Tieng, were thick with VC; and troops there had to deal with a lot of booby traps and snipers. Out on the border, we mainly fought a more conventional war against NVA regulars who were well equipped and clean shaven when they attacked us across the border from their sanctuaries in Cambodia. If they'd had air support and tanks, they would have kicked our butts on a regular basis.

Among the most elite elements of the NVA were the sapper regiments that had been specially trained in night infiltration tactics. We got a brutal introduction to them during early spring when we cycled through an assignment rotation that found us guarding a hellhole called the French Fort at the base of Nui Ba Den, the Black Virgin Mountain.

The Black Virgin sits alone in the middle of the Tay Ninh plain—much as Mount Shasta does on the Sacramento plateau in northern California—and the interior of the mountain was supposedly riddled with enemy hideouts from which they liked to emerge at night and try to knock out some of the big guns of the batteries in the French Fort. The fort was a major fire support base. It held huge guns—eight-inchers and 175mm cannon—along with 155mm and 105mm pieces. And these were the targets the sappers were after.

The first thing we had to do when we got there was dig in, in the new Mole City way. Even though the positions we were occupying had been in place for at least twenty years, we had to rebuild them. The ground was so hard that we could have used TNT to break through it. Somehow we managed to chop out enough to fill sandbags and rim the gun with them. It was an exhausting task, and one evening we were sitting around the pit, bitching about the army, when a major came by. He had heard us and planned to dress us down for our attitude.

"Just whose army do you men think you're in," he demanded, stepping up smartly the way majors always do because, if they don't make light bird by nineteen years, they get cashiered without a pension.

Kumo barely raised his head to acknowledge him, just slid a glance with those cool black eyes of his.

"We're all just USs here, sir," he said. "Don't pay any attention to us."

Kumo may have been a mere three-striper, but he dismissed that major with a smile and a salute. And off the major stumbled, muttering in retreat.

We soon learned that we had more to worry about than rogue officers, once the sappers started showing up in the dead of the night. The sappers could stroll through triple rows of concertina wire like a downtown dude cruising for chicks, and they were just as likely to score. They dressed all in black and popped up at the most unlikely of places, never when you were expecting them.

One of their victims was the lifer E-7 who was in charge of third platoon. He'd just returned from a special compassionate leave. Apparently his marriage was in shambles, his wife talking divorce, so he got a few weeks to fly home and work it out. He came back cheerful enough—I guess they'd retied the knot that binds—but shortly afterward he took a bullet right in the groin. The irony might have seemed more tragic had I not permanently connected him with the order to fire on that bush.

Rocko had a little postgame excitement, as well.

"Woke up and found this little guy pushing a shape charge right in my firing port," he told me one morning. "I was pushing it back out and one of his buddies started pushing him back in with it. Finally had to yank the damn thing right out of his hands and toss it back toward the wire."

What an arm—that's all I could think, remembering the bomb he'd tossed me back at Mole City.

The worst thing about the sappers was the way they got into your mind. If you weren't fucked up before you got there, the French Fort made certain you were by the time you left. Their infiltration skills were such that they might as well have been invisible. Eventually you began to see them everywhere. That must be why the Division constantly changed the infantry unit that guarded the perimeter.

When our three weeks were up, we were all real glad to rotate back to our own base camp. We didn't have any sappers around there—at least any we'd noticed—just good old NVA regulars. Some were the kind who had cut their eyeteeth fighting the French, no doubt—the type, all they knew was war. A few, for sure, could have taught John Wayne a trick or two.

Lots of them were guys like Kumo, myself, and the other USs in our outfit, however. Conscripts. Civilians yanked from their jobs or schools to fight in a war we neither started nor wished to finish. Like us, they were forced to serve as a matter of personal honor and public duty. Knowing that made it damn hard to hate them. I came upon this knowledge rather by accident. One of the guys returning from his one day stand-down brought back a copy of the 25th Division *Tropic Lightning* magazine, presumably because the back cover featured a picture of the memorial service we held at Mole City a couple days after the main battle. Buried inside those glossy pages was an article of startling revelation, the diary of an NVA soldier who had probably passed through Tay Ninh Province just the year before.

Here was a guy going to college in Hanoi, where there was no 2-S deferment. He had no desire to be in a war and, whammo, he gets called into the service. I could identify with that. He could have been me, me him; we were just on opposite sides of the wire.

It didn't take a tremendous act of imagination to realize that he was my karma counterpart. During World War I, French and German troops were said to have visited each other during Christmas truces, walking across the no-man's-land that separated their trench lines and exchanging smokes, pictures, and bottles of whiskey. Then, truce ended, and back to slaughtering each other they went.

Such is the lot of the infantryman. I was sitting in a bleak dusty patrol base, and all I wanted was a milkshake, a shower, and a warm embrace from a blue-eyed East Coast honey who dug rock'n'roll. I guess that made me the lucky one.

The Vietnamese soldier who wrote the journal didn't want anything, anymore. He died in the wire at Ton Son Nhut Air Force Base during the previous year's Tet invasion. They had picked the diary off his dead body. In fact, he might have been killed by someone from my unit. Kumo said the Manchus were there at the time, defending the airstrip, and the scene he described read like my worst combat nightmare.

According to Kumo, when the NVA broke through, they didn't know what to do next, just ran around in circles looking for things to blow up. The mechanized unit Charlie Company was operating with lined up its tracks and blew right down the tarmac, its fifty-calibre machine guns blazing.

"Must of been thousands of them lying out there," Kumo told me, and

I didn't have any reason to doubt him. "Mowed them down as if they were blades of grass."

There was no way of knowing whether or not the soldier had been granted his final wish by the gods of war—to kill one Uncle Soldier. The heated vengeance of that last entry was a sorry commentary on the whole business of warfare. He had started out a nice guy; but by the time he reached Saigon, he had changed.

So had I. I understood how he felt, and that was what bothered me the worst. When I set the magazine down, I felt as if I had taken a journey inside another man's mind—one that I could understand all too well even though he was supposedly the enemy.

I thought about the slaughter that had surrounded him, of his terrible journey down the Ho Chi Minh Trail dodging B-52 strikes, and the march east across Vietnam, when his unit was decimated by gunship attacks and artillery strikes, and the transformation it caused in his nature. What a terrible burden of hatred he was carrying at the end. In some ways he was better off dead.

I wasn't thinking just of him. I thought about the boy we had shot on sweep and about my father, who had made it home from the war and then chose death. I couldn't help but wonder what kind of person I might be when I returned to the world at the end of my tour of duty, if I made it that long.

Dying was starting to make a lot of sense. Too much.

It's hard to describe the level of despair that I felt at that moment. I had never experienced anything like it before in my life. I had many more months left before DEROS, and the weight of those days and weeks yet to be endured crushed down on me with a force so real that I sagged onto the dirt floor of the bunker and gasped dry dusty sobs.

Just about then Francis walked in, blinking like a thirsty hound dog while his eyes adjusted to the dim light.

"Fucking aye, Ab, you hunting centipedes, or what?" he said.

His relentless good ol' boy attitude snapped me back to reality. I realized I must have looked very strange face down in the dirt, so I muttered something about how I thought I'd heard incoming.

"Ain't no fucking goops out there," he said. "Except some old man selling fucking poontang pictures." His eyes bulged. "Man, those baldheaded pussys. The fucking slits really do run the other way. Fucking aye."

By then I was back on my feet and dusting myself off.

"Why don't you go down to the barter point and check it out for real," I suggested.

"No fucking way, Ab. You want me to get fucking brand X. This fellow ain't going to spend the rest of his life on some fucking Japanese island waiting for the sores to heal."

Francis walked out shaking his head, ready to pass on another story about how weird old Ab was.

A few days later I had my chance to go back to Tay Ninh for my one day stand-down. While I was there, I paid a visit to the chaplain. The army always said that if you had a personal problem then that was the thing to do. I spoke to him about the boy, how I had felt such strong feelings for him, and that I was told he had been tossed off the chopper.

He didn't seem to much give a damn. With a terse "People make up stories like that all the time," he dismissed the report about the boy. It was obvious that he was not going to investigate the matter. I couldn't imagine why anyone—especially a guy in my unit—would lie about such a serious thing, so I had just assumed it was true. After talking to the chaplain, I wasn't so sure, though in my heart I still thought it might be. His manner was so abrupt and impersonal that I left without pursuing the matter any further. That chaplain gave me the creeps. The way he looked at me made me feel like I was a bug on the wall. His basic message was clear: Forget it, kid, and get on with the War. I don't want to hear any of that atrocity bullshit.

The next day I returned to Mole City, determined to push my concerns out of my mind. Maybe the chaplain was right, I told myself—not about the boy, but about War. Maybe there were things that were best simply forgotten even though I might not want to, or I might end up like my father, climbing a narrow stairway into the dark attic of the soul. So I decided, without really putting it into words, that I had to go on with the business of being a soldier, the best soldier I could possibly be. The time for being a wise guy, for trying to best the army in the battle of mind games, was over. Sergeant Meredith had it straight all along and had tried to warn me in his quiet way.

Right about then, Kumo left for Hawaii, and not just for R&R. We were all glad to see him go, and not because we weren't going to miss him. He had that special quality about him that made you feel as if you acquired status merely by associating with him. He knew he was good and, by definition, you were too if you were his companion. At the time, I was still in awe of a person who had simple self-respect.

Kumo also represented a link—one of the last—with the previous generation of Suicide Charlie troopers. What unit tradition we had was essentially oral. The bygone "olden" days were always just a DEROS or two away from the dustbin of history. His departure meant additional responsibilities for me, as well. For whatever reason, it was decided by

Stan that I, not Francis, should take over as gunner, despite Francis's two weeks of seniority.

Not much later we left Mole City for good and moved on to other patrol bases. First there was a desolate little base called Delta, where the dust lay so thick that whenever a resupply chopper came in we would form up in a line and dash furiously from one end of camp to the other, racing before the storm. When the chopper took off, we'd line up again and tear off in the other direction.

Our other main form of entertainment at Delta was dodging incoming. The enemy had a fixation on the place, apparently, and they popped a few rounds in almost every single day. We were even gassed at Delta—the only time other than in Basic that I ever tasted the acrid pungency of CS. The enemy mixed it in with some regular high-explosive rounds during one of those spontaneously generated mortar attacks to which we had become so accustomed. We were one confused mob, digging around in the dark of the bunker for our carelessly discarded gas masks. I found Pincush's and handed it to him—a most gracious act, considering the circumstances.

We were hacking and wheezing, our eyes streaming with tears and our throats and lungs seared by the noxious fumes, when someone shouted down to come topside where the air was clear. By then, the incoming had ceased; and as we emerged from underground, we realized to our chagrin that the gas, being heavier than air, had sunk to the lowest point and settled there in our bunker. The purpose of the gas rounds, no doubt, was to drive us up into the open where shrapnel could get us, but we were protected by our inexperience.

Kumo's replacement arrived, in the form of a fellow from Philadelphia named Walter who was so stupid that, when I told him to help us add a second layer of sandbags to the bunker we had inherited, he tried to refuse, arguing that the guys on the plane when he flew over told him that you only needed one. To say that his point of view left me dumbstruck would be an understatement to the point of inverted hyperbole.

Walter had the odd habit of climbing out on top of the bunker during mortar attacks. One night I caught him up there shaking out his pancho liner to the spluttering glow of a parachute flare one of the riflemen had popped after a couple rounds crashed in.

I shouted for him to get down but he refused, saying that this was the only time he could see well enough to complete his housekeeping task. Finally I had to tackle the son of a bitch, whose silhouette would make such an inviting target to a sniper.

One day Walter explained to me that he wasn't worried about dying in the war. In fact, he looked forward to it.

"Christian martyrs go straight to heaven if they die in combat," he said. "Why should I spend all those years trying to live a good enough life to reach Paradise when I could do it right now."

Some arguments are irrefutable, but I wasn't going to let him die on my watch if I could help it. Unless a grenade rolled by. Then we would have been happy to let him hop on it.

Walter didn't hang around for long, though it wasn't the enemy that got him. The army, in its ineffable wisdom, saw fit to send him back home. A compassionate leave—someone said his mother was ill and he was an only child. It made sense to me, however, that they got him out of there. He was the only trooper I ever met with an openly avowed death wish. You couldn't keep somebody like that on the front lines. His wish might come true, and the Minister wouldn't like that at all.

Delta was so close to the border that we could sit on our bunkers at night and see the headlights from convoys of enemy trucks rolling down the Ho Chi Minh Trail. When the B-52s carpet-bombed the trail, the earth shook wildly and we bounced up and down on our air mattresses as if we were floating on choppy waters. That was the closest I ever came to experiencing the kind of bombing raids the NVA soldier wrote about in his diary. It was close enough for me.

B-52 attacks were so awesome that they challenged one's fundamental trust in rationality and sensate experience. People who have been through a serious earthquake say that they never again take the firma of terra quite so for granted, and B-52 attacks must have a similar effect on anybody who has had the misfortune to be underneath one.

Just being nearby, within a click or two, made me question the reliability of the mapmakers, sight manufacturers, and bombardiers. Somehow a couple thousand meters no longer seemed to be as great a distance as it did when I was humping across it, and not nearly a wide enough buffer zone. The explosions were so massive that they shrunk the very concept of length the way darkness does, when a lighted object appears so much closer than it would during the daytime.

They didn't call it "Rolling Thunder" for nothing.

The longer I stayed in-country and the more I witnessed the firepower the American military poured at them, the greater admiration I gained for the courage of the enemy soldiers. Sometimes, such as at Mole City, it was said that they dug mass graves before the attack. Their own graves, as the case was. This was not an attitude that I, nor many of my comrades, could relate to very easily. We were in the War to stay alive, not die. Twelve months and out. They were in it so deep that there was only one way out, and it was down the long dark tunnel.

One day outside Delta we captured a grizzled old Vietnamese in a place where he wasn't supposed to be and brought him back to base camp. Intelligence took him down into a bunker and wired his balls to a field phone. Then they cranked the juice and electricity flowed through his testicles. This was a common, nonfatal way of grabbing an interrogatee's attention. Those twelve-volt batteries carried quite a jolt.

Afterward they left him sitting in the sun, wondering when he would be going back down, or taking a bullet in the head. Schell, the fellow who had been hit by rocket shrapnel, went over and gave him a cigarette and a drink of water even though we had been ordered to leave him alone.

"The guy's a human being first, and an enemy second," Schell said, and I had to agree with him.

Orders or no orders, it was the right thing to do.

Not everybody shared Schell's sense of common humanity. There was a big market in the rear for dead gook pictures. It seemed that the further away they were from the real thing, the more bizarre became men's fascination for death and mutilation. Some guys took the pictures and sold them to the truck drivers, cooks, and clerks back in Tay Ninh and Cu Chi for a little extra beer money when they were on R&R, but I never did. I always felt that those fierce little men deserved more respect than to become trophies in some REM's photo album.

One of the more bizarre scenes we ever witnessed involved sweeping an area after a bombing strike. It had been leafletted by communist propagandists. The ground was strewn with crude mimeographed flyers that told us we were tools of the capitalist system and fighting and dying so that evil bosses back in America could get rich on our blood. Some of us kept them for souvenirs, but it was hard to take their suggestion to defect very seriously. Where we supposed to march out into the jungle and throw ourselves into the arms of our proletarian brethren? No way.

It was Us against Them, like it or not, and that was how it was going to remain until the bosses said otherwise. A lot about the War made little sense, but not that much had since the day I'd stepped off the bus at Fort Benning, Georgia.

One thing that did amaze me was the attitude of some of the ARVN (Army of the Republic of Vietnam) units we occasionally teamed up with. Some were pretty tough. We shared a night perimeter with ARVN marines, and nobody lost too much sleep over it. Regular troops and Popular Forces were another matter. They were generally referred to as

"Marvin the Arvin" and "Puffs," and their commanders were frequently known to disengage from enemy contact at 5 P.M. and return to their base, leaving an American unit behind to keep up the good battle. When they were on patrol, some Arvins would walk along, joking and laughing, even holding hands, as if the War meant nothing to them.

Gradually, I began to realize that the situation in Vietnam was very ambiguous, at best. No one was certain of the loyalties of any of the Vietnamese. The new Nixon administration in Washington had been elected in part on the claim of having a "secret plan" to end the War, and it was still a secret to all of us out in the field. We didn't know if we were supposed to want to fight, or not. All we were certain of was that, if attacked, we would respond. Mole City had proven that.

Despite the incident with the boy, Mole City remained my touchstone. I never forgot the bodies of the American soldiers I had carried off on the morning after the attack, and the terror I had felt when the AKs opened up. Memories had been etched into my soul with the acid of bitterness. Like the burning hot shrapnel from a white phosphorous round, they burrowed deeper and deeper into the marrow until they became part of the very substance of my being.

Occasionally, when I was very tired or unusually depressed, my thoughts would wander and my inward eye would catch a glimpse of the image of that boy on the border—the helpless, horrified look in his eyes as he stared down the barrels of our M-16s. Then I would see him spinning through the air like the rotor blades on a Huey. And if it was late at night and very quiet, I could almost hear him scream.

─── 12 ───

New Mexico

I sit here on a mound of clay, my rifle in one hand, a child's hand in the other. Soft and small, curled inside my grasp, I think of it as a talisman or an amulet. I rub it with my thumb across his knuckles, my fingers pressed against his fleshy palm so plump with infancy.

I don't know his name, he doesn't know mine. We are looking at pictures in the magazine that lies across my knees, he turning the pages in his clumsy way, me uttering dumb statements, stupid statements such as "Paris. Luxembourg. New Mexico."

He knows only this small plot of earth that we sit on, that we walk in half a day's time, from which we can look out and his tender untrained infant's eye can see the hazy scope of bunkers and cannons and his small round ears can tell the sound of jet motors, the scream of tortured air he knows well.

I name him Wun. Thieu might be closer, I suppose, but he seems so young to me, younger than I can remember ever having been—and yet, to think what he knows when so young. At two, he will be far wiser than I am at twenty. Already he can dive as fast as a jet, a rocket, a howitzer shell. He can scream with the sky. And he can laugh. Laugh like a Greek god must laugh looking down from Mt. Olympus and seeing us silly Americans, foolish as Daedalus, foolish as Paris, as Agamemnon and Ulysses.

As foolish as the publishers of the magazine we are looking at, with its lovely mannequinlike models and slick pictures of scenic marvels that seem so unreal juxtaposed against the ragged children who hang out at the dump. As foolish as the riders of helicopters who fly above the base camp on the lookout for the kids who collect here beside our refuse piles, where they dig for sugar packets and stale biscuits to supplement their diet of mother's milk, bamboo shoots, and the spicy meat of rats and dogs.

"Paris," I say, and point to a picture of the Eiffel Tower, glistening in morning wet.

"Arctic," I say, and point to a seal, fat with blubber and sleek as steel. Sweat drops from my face and dissolves into the print.

"Snow," I say, pointing at the page.

"Snow," he says, pointing to the seal. "Seal," pointing to the tower, rubbing the picture as if he knew it was meant to be rubbed. We rub it together, gloss, sweat, and fingers dissolving all into one until the tower and the snow and the seal are well mixed together.

From Delta we moved on to another base camp, one that I called New Mexico because the arid late-dry-season terrain reminded me of the Southwest. At sunset the sky radiated random colors, pink and orange pastels, turquoise, and many others, as if the sun were a rapidly spinning multifaceted precious stone. One evening I saw a splotch of green—a rare phenomenon occasionally witnessed in the tropics. It appeared like a vision created by desire, a whimsy of green that caught a glint of the sun and reflected there ever so briefly. I looked for it many times after that, but never snatched a glimpse of it again.

When dusk fell, the outlines of trees and shrubs looked to me like cactuses. Even though it was as flat there as everywhere else in Tay Ninh Province, off in the distance I imagined I could see mountains. Mountains that I longed to climb. Mountains that were capped by glaciers, where a cold wind swirled and no vegetation grew but a few hardy stunted evergreens.

It was April now, and I'd missed winter. I'd passed my first full season in Vietnam. American season, that is. In Vietnam, I learned, there really are only two seasons: wet and dry. We'd had a bit of rain in early spring, just a cloudburst now and again. They called it the mini-monsoon and it didn't amount to much. Now the grass was beginning to fade; a brown tinge was spreading across the land like a blight.

I was glad to be out of Delta, which was such a barren dust pit. New Mexico was a well-established army base with a resident battery of 155s that had civilized the wilderness. It had all the accoutrements, including a large and heavily frequented barter point where I had my one Vietnam Sex Experience. It also had a dump that was enclosed in barbed wire and that we had to guard from the children of a nearby village.

They were a treacherous crew, those village children who hung out there in search of food. Command said they were secreting supplies for the Viet Cong, squirreling away food, shell casings, and empty tin cans for booby traps. The myth was that we litter-conscious American soldiers walking along a jungle path would bend down under our heavy packs and pick up discarded cans of C-rations. All as part of a "Keep Vietnam Beautiful" program, I suppose. I felt certain that the Brass's concern was more of a different issue. Just didn't look good to their lifer eyes to see little children scrambling after our refuse.

For the kids, the dump represented their war-zone version of a mall. They poked and dug, ferreting out edible scraps from our discarded rations. Sugar packets were especially prized finds, but the children were no snobs. Even C-ration tins of ham and eggs that we GIs tossed out with scorn landed on their must-eat list.

Most of the guys felt they were as harmless as I did, and didn't mind them rifling through our trash. The light bird in the LOACH saw it differently, of course, so we were assigned dump guard duty and ordered to keep them out.

Some soldiers showed real initiative at this task. A few kids got shot at, and one took a hit from an M-79 slug. Another needed nearly fifty stitches after a star-cluster flare cut up his thigh. The medics sewed him back up and, as soon as he could get around with a cane, he was back at the dump. A fanatical enemy supporter, no doubt.

The dump was surrounded by concertina wire, so it was no small feat for the kids to get in there in the first place. New Mexico had a deuce and a half that served as a dump truck. Each morning when it brought out its load, the kids would take up positions beside the dirt trail. As the truck neared the gate, they would swarm to its sides. The driver would put the pedal to the metal and blow on through while the guard held the gate open. Kids would leap for the running boards and tailgate, others would try to flash through the narrow opening on either side of the truck. It was deadly sport. Great fun until a little girl took a direct hit from the dump truck.

To avoid accidents, I let the kids enter in shifts. An early complaint of Command was that kids would get their feet torn up by jagged tin and broken glass so I only let in the ones with shoes on. They'd dig for the goodies and bring them back out to share with everyone else. To answer the other complaint, I made them eat the stuff on the spot. That way the children couldn't be accused of hoarding for the VC.

Not on my shift, anyway.

Dump guard duty was my one chance to get to know the locals. I would sit outside the wire enclosure and visit with the children. The little ones would sit in my lap while we leafed through old photography magazines. I'd point out pictures of places they would most likely never see: the Alps, rhinoceroses in Uganda, fjords in Norway. They loved it, and I did too.

Those were precious moments, holding little hands and chatting in one-word sentences. But the Minister of Misery must have been watching, and he didn't like what he saw. After a few days, I was relieved of trash-dump guard duty and nearly transferred out of Suicide Charlie.

Duty was slow at New Mexico. Patrols were infrequent, and we were not called on often to fire. The area must have been pacified, but Command felt the artillery squadron required at least token protection.

One afternoon, with time to kill because I was no longer wanted at the dump, I took a stroll to the barter point. It felt a bit strange, walking outside the wire without a weapon. It was one of the few times I did it when I was in the field.

It was a well-worn path that led to the shaded spot where the camp followers sold their wares. As I approached, I could see half a dozen women or more, some of whom had very small children in their charge. The remarkable clarity in the unpolluted air added a vibrancy to the bright colors of the clothes worn by the prostitutes who hung out at the barter point. They were dressed in red and yellow blouses and ink-black slacks that were split above the ankle like pedal pushers are. Watching the mama-sans flitter about, chasing children and fixing meals, they looked to me like holiday kites bobbing at the end of a tether on a breezy day.

Some of the women spoke excellent pidgin English, and one was even current on American politics. With her, I discussed the comparative merits of presidents Johnson and Nixon. She thought well of Johnson for committing American troops to the war and was disappointed that he had chosen not to run for reelection. Nixon and his "secret plan" were a bit of an enigma to her. Then again, she was not alone on that account.

I didn't tell her about my involvement at the Agnew rally.

Most of the women were not there for serious conversation, however. They were there to earn a living the only way they knew how. They were boom-boom girls, as the GIs called them, and the going rate was five dolla' MPC.

MPC was military payment currency, funny money printed by the army to slow down black-market action on greenbacks. Every so often, the military would roll over the currency. When that happened, we could cash in up to $200 MPC; anything more was worthless. It probably did not affect the big-time operators back in Saigon, who most certainly got

the word in advance, but the little people at the barter point, or any GI who'd won a big pot the night before, lost out.

It took a couple of days for the new scrip to make it to the field, so, for those brief periods, the barter point lived up to its name. Currency became consumer goods—especially cigarettes and soap. It is to the Vietnamese people's eternal credit that at those times soap was considered more valuable than tobacco, by a ratio of one bar to two packs. How many American nicotine freaks would have made a similar distinction, I wondered.

As I walked through the barter point, I passed a few soda boys. They were leaning against their mopeds with the proprietary air of American teenagers proudly posing beside their hotrods outside a hamburger joint. Further on, a couple of GIs were fraternizing. The boom-boom girls had their favorites, and I was not one of them. I never gave them any business and I smoked Pall Malls, which they wouldn't even take as a gift. Winstons and Marlboros, it seems, are worldwide favorites. I smoked Kurt Vonnegut's brand of coffin nails not because I wished to congregate with particular people, but because nobody else wanted them. I could have all I desired. Kools, Winstons, and Marlboros were gone in a flash when a new box of goodies arrived in the field; Pall Malls lasted forever.

I shuffled up to the crowd, nervous as any underage booze buyer worried about getting carded. I had sex on my mind and no idea how one solicited a prostitute. Awkward and uncertain, I tried to make small talk with the women, but my courage failed me quickly and I would have returned to base camp an abysmal failure had not one of the oldest women there—a thirtyish mama-san—not taken me by the hand and pulled me away from the pack. She led me toward a clump of bushes that apparently served as a bedroom suite. Unlike some of the younger prettier girls, she was dressed entirely in black except for a conical straw hat tied beneath her chin with a bright red ribbon.

After we eased down a narrow path through the bushes and emerged into a small clearing, she stopped and turned toward me. I reached down and untied her hat, then bent to kiss her betel-nut-stained red lips. (Many Vietnamese women chewed betel nuts, a mild nicotine addictive that rots teeth by middle age.) She pulled back from me and quickly undressed in a very businesslike fashion. Her skin was a motley brown, splotched with large moles. Her eyes were the color of burnt umber, her legs short and bowed, and her breasts small and wrinkled as overripe avocados.

I started to undress and, business being business, she told me I'd have to wear a rubber. The Trojan would cost an extra quarter. I anted up after

fumbling through the pockets of my pants, which were hanging about my ankles. The romantic chauvinist in me demanded that she put it on.

"Mama-san no touch smelly dick," she uttered in undisguised disdain.

When I indicated otherwise, she jumped back into her clothes and stomped out of the bushes. That was it for me—not even a hard-on. I pulled up my pants and slouched sheepishly back to base camp, my Vietnam Sex Experience drawn to an unsated conclusion.

Later that day or another one soon following—days had a way of blending together in Vietnam with so little to differentiate them other than the rising and setting of the sun—I was strolling through New Mexico and I heard the low strains of the Doors' classic song "Light My Fire." To an old hippie-type like myself surrounded pretty much by country'n'western fans, the sweet music of rock'n'roll might have been a bubbling spring to a parched sojourner wandering in the desert.

I followed the music right inside an artillery emplacement, six-foot-high sandbag walls that encircled a gun. Several troopers were sitting there, grooving out to the music, which was being supplied by a little battery-powered record player. Nobody paid any attention to me as I wandered in and sat down; they just included me in the circle and passed along the number they were smoking. The whole scene appeared so natural it never even occurred to me to worry that marijuana was, technically at least, illegal. They sure weren't uptight about it, and this was their base camp.

Sunlight was filtering down through the palm trees and the sounds were mellow. Nobody talked much, just laid back and listened. It was the best music I'd ever heard. I guess the taste was so much sweeter because I'd been hungry for so long.

When the song ended I moved along as quietly as I had arrived, grateful for having snatched off a piece of a dream. The euphoria didn't last long. Back at my squad area, Stan met me with the news that I was going to be transferred.

Stan was getting short by then, and we had been discussing who should replace him as squad leader, Francis or me. I thought I should be the one. They had, after all, bypassed the normal order of seniority and made me gunner when Kumo had left. Stan had implied that he agreed with me and had said that he would bring the matter up with Sarge. Now, it seemed, I was learning the hard lesson Sergeant Meredith had once tried to pass on in more subtle ways. He must have remembered my ill-chosen remarks to Same-same concerning authority and the right of command. While I still rejected mindless obedience, I did accept the importance of leadership in critical circumstances such as combat, and I

wanted to be in that position because I cared about the men around me. I thought I could do a better job of keeping them alive.

The question of succession became meaningless once the word of the transfer arrived, however. I no longer cared what position I held, I just didn't want to leave my unit.

For the first time since that brief lapse the morning after at Mole City, I stood outside the bunker and wiped a few tears from the corners of my eyes. To be forced to leave my unit seemed terribly unfair, but Stan told me I had no choice. I was to join a special detachment stationed at the top of Nui Ba Den.

As the highest point around for many many miles, the Black Virgin's tactical value was self-evident. At its craggy windswept peak squatted a small American communications post that maintained an uneasy coexistence with the enemy troops who lived inside the mountain.

Nui Ba Den was a religious shrine and, as such, it was supposedly off limits for artillery and air strikes. Various attempts to storm it had cost many lives over the years, including those of quite a few Manchus. Bravo Company had made a charge up the hill the year before in a joint operation with a mechanized unit—probably the 4th of the 23rd—and only a handful of survivors had staggered back down after walking into a nasty ambush. In August 1968, attackers had snuck out of the honeycombed caves and, under the cover of thick clouds and a heavy wind, assaulted the com base at the top of the three-thousand-foot-high mountain, killing or wounding nearly thirty soldiers. The following winter they had performed a macabre sequel—Night on Nui Ba Den II—and rumor was they were thinking of doing it again.

The word also was that the Black Virgin held an NVA hospital and in-country R&R center for battle-weary enemy troops. I'd gotten a good look at Nui Ba Den while we were stationed at the French Fort and its barren wastes did little to incite my interest in being stationed there, even if it meant being part of what I was informed would be an elite unit of men with near-perfect records.

Command had decided that the only way to break the vicious deadly cycle of successful sneak attacks on troops who had grown careless due to inactivity and boredom locked there on the mountain top was to create a crack outfit, and my record was spotless. I also was a gunner with six months left in country, one of the slots Charlie Company had been *suggested* to fill.

The next morning I took the early chopper into Tay Ninh, as dispirited as I had ever felt. I stalled around company HQ for a few days, delaying the inevitable. I talked to "Short Round," a former platoon leader and now a first louie company executive officer in charge of the rear; but he said I had to go, thank you, and have a nice time up on the mountain. So I trucked on over to the heliport with my gear on the day we were to ship out. As I was waiting to board a chopper for the ascent to hell, as I saw it, I told the guy next to me that I didn't want to go. He said I should talk to the first sergeant, that he'd been told this new unit was all volunteer. I sucked up my courage, stalked into the orderly room, and told the grizzled E-9 in charge that I wanted to have words with him.

He froze me with a look that would have melted ice in Alaska.

"Make it quick, trooper," he demanded.

"It's the mountain," I stuttered. "I don't want to go there."

"Then get the hell out of here," he snorted. "This is an all-volunteer outfit. If you don't want us, then we sure as hell don't want you. Get your gear and get back to your unit, god damn it."

I didn't wait around for him to change his mind.

"Wait till I talk to your Ex-O," I heard him mutter as I hurried out the door.

I figured I'd better tell Short Round first. I fled back to my compound and gave him the news. He was disappointed, mainly because he would now have to come up with another "volunteer." But I think he understood. He had been a platoon leader at Mole City and he knew what our next assignment was going to be. He probably believed that he was doing me a favor, whether I realized it or not.

Maybe he was. Until that transfer I hadn't understood how important my unit had become to me. I cared about Stan and Pincush, Melvin, even Francis. I cared about something else, as well. It mattered to me that I was part of Company C, the 4th of the 9th. Remarkably enough, I had developed loyalty to my unit. For whatever it was worth, I had laced myself to the mast of the good ship *Suicide Charlie* and I planned to ride out the storm right there.

While I was at Tay Ninh, I learned that the Wolfhounds had gotten hit again. Not satisfied with one Diamond, they had built two more, and both Diamonds II and III had met with ground assaults, the first on April 5, the second on the 15th. Williamson's Force Fed Fire Support had apparently worked, as losses were reported to have been minimal relative to NVA casualties, but the battles made it clear that the enemy had not yet given up the fight in Zone III.

When I got back to New Mexico with the news, Stan was gone. I didn't even get a chance to say good-bye. We must have crossed flights. In my absence, Francis had taken over the squad. It was a done deed and, somewhat reluctantly, I had to admit that it was for the best. I was a good gunner, and that's where I belonged. Stan had trained me well and I was lucky to have been his pupil.

Stan was the last of the old guys who had seen it all with Charlie Company. He and Kumo had been my teachers. Cool under fire, brave when bravery was a necessity for survival, stable in the midst of chaos, they, along with Harry, formed a triumvirate that represented the ideal of an infantryman to me. Stan's departure created a vacuum that Francis, Pincush, and I had to fill. We were the veterans now, and it was time for us to assume the mantle of leadership. I felt as if I was walking in the shadows of giants. Soon our mettle would be tested. Word came down to prepare to ship out. We were going back to the border to build a new base camp, one so close to the border that it would be called Frontier City.

We were going out after the NVA, just like at Mole City. No other companies would be joining in our expedition. This time, Suicide Charlie was going out alone.

Terrifying though the assignment might be, I was damn glad to be going with them.

13

The Battle of Frontier City

Tonight.

This is the night they are coming.

The Fool on the Hill has spotted movement. Enemy troops by the hundreds, perhaps two or three thousand. Atop the thirty-foot tower he can see well into Cambodia. The border is just a couple thousand yards away. Beyond it is COSVN, the HQ for the Southern Command of the entire North Vietnamese Army. The 272nd Regiment is heading our way.

The waiting begins.

Seconds tick by. Minutes. Pieces of an hour.

Tonight.

Everybody knows it. Pincush, Francis, Melvin. The guys on the bunker line. Major Harry Ray: radio name, the Fool on the Hill. He's the guy in the tower. We call him the Mad Manchu.

Tonight we find out if Suicide Charlie can live down its name.

Yesterday we hit the ground digging. Rockets and mortars welcomed us to the border. Hardpan so tough you couldn't drive a spike into it with a sledge-hammer, and we were on our knees swinging a pick, digging in an inch at a time. Dropped off in the neutral zone, right across from the NVA main force.

Human bait, that's what we are, set out here like a lamb tied to a stake. Since yesterday morning the enemy soldiers have been sharpening their bayonets, anticipating the kill.

Tonight.

A Shadow gunship lumbers in from Tay Ninh and circles outside the perimeter. For the moment, we are safe. They won't hit us with the Shadow up *there. Time to piss and smoke a cigarette. This is it. Soon as that Shadow leaves.*

If the army really was trying to wipe out Suicide Charlie, then it came up with a perfect place to do it. We hopped down from the choppers to find ourselves in a barren no-man's-land devoid of vegetation other than some stunted grass and a few parched shrubs. At least Mole City had some trees.

There was plenty of jungle cover off to the west, a quick hop across the border into the sanctuary where the NVA troops were relaxing, but here on the plain so late in the dry season everything was brown, thirsty, and forbidding. Positively uncivilized. I guess that's why they called it Frontier City.

A perfect place to die, I was thinking as I unslung my rucksack the morning of April 25, 1969, and took a swig from my canteen. The sun was so hot I could almost hear my skin sizzle. I took a long drink and tucked my canteen into the shadow of my pack. Another flight of choppers dropped off more of my company. The dust was still swirling from prop wash when rockets started coming in.

"Welcome to Frontier City," some wise guy was saying, using shrapnel for an introduction.

I was hoping he wouldn't show up in person too soon.

There is one preferred direction in the average infantryman's range of movement, down, straight down, and I was aiming in that direction. We picked and shoveled and sweated until pools of mud filled our shallow holes in the hardpan. We didn't stop to pose for group pictures when the *Time* and AP folks popped in for a quick—very quick—photo op.

Command was talking tanks out there on the border, the infantryman's vision of Armageddon. I parked my pit right behind Rocko's 90MM recoilless rifle emplacement. They'd have to go through him to get to me and I didn't envy them one bit.

Rocko looked like a commemorative statue of the American Man-At-Arms, with the bicep definition of a character right out of a World War II combat comic book. As George Frazier might have written, he had duende.

I don't know if the bullet Rocko took in his right arm ruined his chances for a pro career, but he had returned to the field in a hurry and I was glad to see him. At Frontier City they were talking twenty to one, as well as tanks, and we knew we'd need all our all-stars in the lineup on game day.

At Mole City, it took the NVA four days to hit us. But now we were closer. Near enough for them to hear our radios play. I hoped they didn't mind the station our dial was set on.

The numbers were all on their side and I didn't feel good about it all. They'd hit Diamonds II and III earlier in the month, knocking down a few Wolfhounds in the process, and I couldn't see why it was so necessary to provoke them into another attack. Mole City was bad, but this read like an infantryman's worst version of a horror story. The NVA never seemed to attack unless they had us badly outnumbered. Numerical superiority was their chief military asset. Ours was firepower.

The technology that American society had developed to kill people was truly awesome. We had M-16s, napalm, white phosphorous, HE (high explosives), Phantom jets, ten-thousand-pound bombs, 90mm recoilless rifles armed with fleshette rounds (each shell held thousands of tiny metal arrows), 60mm and fifty-calibre machine guns, rocket-propelled grenades, eight-inch guns with projectiles the size of small people, claymore mines made of plastic explosive riddled with hundreds of bb-sized shot, Cobra gunships armed with mini-guns that fired a thousand rounds a minute, and, most fiercesome of all, the Shadow. Just to name a few.

Given that kind of weaponry, a unit doesn't come by the name Suicide Charlie easily.

Take one hundred guys, whittle 'em down to fifteen or twenty, bring in a new bunch, kill off a whole lot more, keep this up for several months, throw them into battle against vastly superior enemy units, take the survivors and drop them out on the border where they can watch enemy munitions trucks high rolling down the Ho Chi Minh Highway, put up a flashing sign advertising American boys for slaughter, wholesale, season lightly with a few promotion-minded gung-ho officers, and, presto, you've got it, combat salad, heavy on the greens.

Frontier City was the army's way of saying thanks for the memories to Company C of the 4th Bn., 9th Inf. Bde. So much for sentiment.

By the second night we were about as ready as we were ever going to be to absorb a direct hit from a reinforced regiment of crack NVA troops. We'd built our bunkers, stockpiled rounds and ammo, cleaned our weapons and written last letters home. Now it was all up to the Gods of War.

About 10 P.M. the Fool on the Hill called down from the tower.

"We know they're coming but we don't want them to know that we know. Everybody act natural. Make some noise. Turn up your radios."

This had to be a first in infantry annals, an event made possible by the transistor revolution. There was only one station out there—AFRN—and at that moment it was broadcasting "Harry, the Hairy Ape," a novelty song by Ray Stevens, the man who brought us Clive the Camel and Ahab the Arab. Everybody turned up their radios at the same time and the base camp was rocking.

"Ohhhh heeeeeey heeeeeey ohhhhhhh heeeeeeeeey," Ray Stevens was yodeling as a couple thousand NVA troops from their elite 9th Division closed in on us. As they neared the base, artillery rounds from Tay Ninh started whistling overhead and booming down outside the wire. All through the day, the Fool on the Hill had directed numerous spotting rounds of artillery from the fire support bases. "Defconning" this was called, defining and reconnoitering an area by fire so that the guns knew their coordinates ahead of time. Popcorn lit up all along the horizon as the eight-inchers and 175s starting dropping. An hour passed. The artillery let up. The enemy crept closer. The noose tightened.

A Shadow cruised in and started blasting enemy positions. Shadow dropped parachute flares and knocked down a couple hundred thousand rounds in about fifteen minutes while we all watched with supreme admiration. There was no way we'd get hit while the Shadow was in the air. The converted C-47 cargo plane had four mini-guns and an armory's load of ammunition. You could have used it to cut grass and done a pretty neat job with it. Only thing was, it couldn't circle forever. And once it left, we couldn't expect to see another.

Just about midnight, I felt an overwhelming need to pee and hopped out of the pit and sauntered over to a more private spot, there to do my business. Just as I was finishing up, Shadow disappeared. This was not good timing. Hastily tucking away my most important appendage, I heard the screech of an incoming rocket. I raced toward my position, looking back over my shoulder to see the impact. It was close, real close, and I leaped for the pit, getting a boost from the blast. I was floating through the air slowly, so it seemed, ever so slowly. As I fell toward the parapet, I could see the blue-white flame of the rocket splash spreading out through the night like the unfolding wings of a beautiful phosphorescent butterfly. I landed in the pit beside the gun still unbuttoned but all in one piece and happy to be there. I never did measure exactly how far I leaped, but it was a very long ways.

Just as at Mole City, rockets, mortars, and RPGs started crashing in, lots of them. Hundreds upon hundreds. We dove into the bunker and waited out the storm. Kumo and Stan weren't in there with us this time to lead the charge back out. This time it was me and Francis and Mike, we were going to have to provide the leadership. After surviving Mole City, we knew this was going to be a fight to the finish. Reinforcements were so far away that any breach of the perimeter meant certain death for all.

During that initial barrage, the enemy had plenty of time to close in on our bunker line and we had plenty of time to think about our situation. If anything, the fire was heavier than it had been at Mole City. My terror that first night of combat had been primordial, innocent; it had issued from within without any basis in experience. This time it was different. Worse. I had little faith that we could hold off such a massive unit and I knew what it meant to be overrun. I had carried the bodies, seen the wounds, heard the screams. Felt the fear. It was all too real.

I could only hope that, this time, fire support would not let us down. But an attack on the mountain could destroy communications, and a major assault on any of the other patrol bases in the region would divert much of our support, leaving us to fend for ourselves in the face of a well-armed and vastly larger enemy unit.

My empathy for the enemy that I had felt after reading the diary of the NVA soldier, as well my thoughts concerning the boy we shot on sweep, lost its hold on me as I sweated out the initial attack in that dark dusty bunker we had tossed together in only a few hours' time. It was replaced by anger, a cold fire that burned all the deeper for its lack of heat. I wanted to fight, to get even, to seize control of the situation and replace the impotence of cringing in terror with the strike of an iron-clad fist, to fire and fire again, and again. To drive out these apparitions by the force of my will and destroy the enemy even if it meant that, to do it, I had to kill.

When the barrage at last lifted, there was no hesitation before I charged back out to the gun. The rattle of rifle and machine-gun fire deafened us as we took our positions and prepared to return fire.

The Fool on the Hill had survived the incoming, and the Mad Manchu was radioing down target locations. Tracers were bouncing off the tower. Melvin said it looked like a sparkler on the Fourth of July. It was hard to understand how it held up under that fusillade, but as long as it did I was going to follow the spotter's instructions.

Francis started relaying aiming coordinates. I was peering out through the smoke and dust, trying to focus on my sighting stakes through the swirling chaos. Constant explosions lit up the darkness, the stakes bucked and swayed, but I had driven them in deep and they didn't fall.

We entered a firing frenzy, dropping rounds as fast as the ammo bearers could bring them, trying to help the guys on the bunker line break up the massive ground assault. A sapper unit broke through the wire and two 105mm cannons that had been deployed with us lowered their barrels and fired at point-blank range. Captain Pulliman caught word of the breakthrough and raced over to the endangered area, leading the counterfire with an M-60. He was determined that there would be no third platoon sacrifice this time.

As the fighting roared all around me, I lost all consciousness of the sounds and scenes of the battle. I was totally concentrating on my gun. We started firing marking rounds for a fleet of helicopter gunships, and accuracy was critical to ensure that we got the most out of their assistance. Inside my bubble of space, there existed only the gun, my stakes, and a voice calling out coordinates as I spun the sight to the proper reading, found the tiny red lights blinking on the poles, and levelled the sight horizontally and vertically, making fast fine adjustments until the lights were lined up one right behind the other so tightly that they looked like one. Once that was done, I nodded for Pincush to drop the rounds. The entire process took only seconds.

Sometimes, as I peered at my stakes, explosions would shatter the darkness. Back blasts from Rocko's 90mm recoilless, I figured, reassured. I hadn't forgotten the rumor of tanks. Totally exposed from the waist up as I was, I didn't care to consider the other explanations for the explosions. The close encounter with the rocket had been enough for one night.

Whenever I looked up, I checked to ensure that the tower was still standing. Green tracers and the red glow of RPGs sliced toward it, but Major Ray had on his full body armor that night, and must have swallowed a double dose of immortality potion. As long as he was calling the shots, I was going to follow his directions. He had a much better view.

The Manchu slogan is "Keep Up the Fire," which we did. Superior firepower is meaningless without the will to use it, and the men of Suicide Charlie were relentless in their determination to exploit their advantage. Artillery from the big guns was roaring overhead and we were blasting away with everything we had. We were building a wall of steel but still the NVA kept charging. After a while, I began to wonder how much longer we could hold out. Soon we would need resupply and there was no way a Chinook was going to descend through that fusillade. It would have disintegrated in midair. We all knew that Frontier City was a couple of breeched bunkers away from disappearing under a flood of enemy troops, and the longer they maintained the assault, the more bitter tasted the acrid smoke-clouded air.

"They must have a soldier factory on the other side of the border," Pincush said. "And the assembly line is working overtime."

I knew what he meant.

Melvin dashed into the pit with another load of rounds.

"Ain't much more in there," he announced, his once smooth chubby face now taut and deeply creased with dirt-smeared lines.

I worried about how the guys on the bunker line were holding up and started to think about joining them. I still had lots of ammo left for my M-16 and, if it came to it, I had a bayonet.

"I wonder if they defconned our bunker," Francis said, only half in jest.

We weren't dug in like we had been at Mole City. The ground was too hard and there hadn't been time. What we did have was a high berm pushed up by a dozer the previous afternoon, and a clear field of fire the first hundred or so yards outside the bunker line.

They wouldn't be able to charge straight out of the trees like they had in December. On the other hand, their supply lines were a lot shorter and we were going to run out of materiel long before they would. By two or three in the morning we were all thinking Mole City II, but this time Command had a surprise for us.

While I was waiting for Pincush to strip another round, I heard a faint putt-putt-putt, at first so low that it barely penetrated the din of the battle. I strained to listen, not daring to believe my ears. The sound grew louder until it could not be mistaken.

Shadow!

Suddenly it was above us, dropping flares and blasting away with its mini-guns. I stood beside my gun and smiled. Those poor little yellow bastards were going to get it now, and I didn't mind at all. It was a beautiful sight, that Shadow, a vision of deliverance. Fighting around the perimeter really intensified. The assault troops must have figured they would be safer inside than out. We poured out the fire and smashed the attack.

Several Phantom fighter planes roared overhead, swooping down and spitting bullets at the fleeing soldiers, chasing them all the way back to Cambodia. Off along the horizon, the sky came alive with ack-ack as the jets closed on the main enemy base camps. I'd never seen antiaircraft fire before and settled back to enjoy the show.

It was Miller Time.

We helped blast the distant enemy positions with our mortars, firing charge nines due west, well into Lon Nol land. It was the NVA HQ that Command was really interested in, and jets and artillery pounded it all night long. Never mind that the *Stars & Stripes* reported the next day that no American fire crossed the Cambodian border. We were doing just that with our little 81s. The big stuff travelled much farther.

When dawn broke, we went out and looked for bodies. The official count was 213. Body counts being what they were—statistical hallucinations—who knows what losses the NVA really suffered. For certain, there were still a lot around. Thirteen dead were found in one cluster and it looked as if a mortar round had taken them out. I kind of thought of them as mine. Certainly, there were plenty to go around—and this time, somebody else did the undertaking.

Oh, those sorry brave little NVA regulars. When I saw the carnage our firepower had wreaked, I had to admit that they used up more courage lacing their boots in the morning than I did through a whole night of battle.

Our losses were none. Zero. Zilch. Nine wounded, none serious. Frontier City was one of the most lopsided battles in the history of the war. It was the ultimate vindication of General Williamson's bait-and-switch tactics. Suicide Charlie got even for a lot of humiliation that night. I can't say I believed in the war—though, in the flush of victory, it made some sense to me right then—or that I truly hated the enemy. But as the sun rose over Frontier City, I didn't shed any tears for the NVA troops who had crossed paths with my outfit one time too many.

On the way back in, I stopped by Rocko's bunker. I figured he had some gratitude coming his way.

"Thanks, man," I said. "Made me feel good all night seeing those back blasts from the 90."

"Shit, Norm," he replied. "Gun jammed on the second round. Tossed it over the berm in case it exploded. See it out there. Time to clean it up and get it working in case they come again tonight. Those were 82s you were looking at. They were firing your way all night long."

Then he laughed the way you can laugh when you are six and a half feet tall and your torso looks like a contour map of the Rocky Mountains.

Weeelll. A couple hours later I was still standing in my shit waiting for the trembling to stop when a guy came out from Division. Wanted to know if I'd like to become a reporter for the *Tropic Lightning News*.

It didn't take me too long to get my gear together, slip into something fresh, and hop that chopper back to Tay Ninh. That magic day had finally arrived, the one those guys back at the *Recorder* had told me would come.

The army had remembered that I could write.

I was thinking hootch girls, cold beer, swimming pools and first-run movies, full course meals and massage parlors. I was also thinking, if the truth be told, no Frontier City, no NVA, no more nightly terror.

So I left behind Rocko and Sergeant Meredith, Francis and Pincush and Melvin, and about a hundred other guys with whom I'd fought for my life, and returned to Tay Ninh to bop around with a bunch of nerdy REMs who hardly ever picked up a gun, who slept on cots and had clean young Vietnamese women as live-in maids, who ate chow at cafeterias at real tables, sitting in chairs like at a Morrison's or a McDonald's, complete with little trays to carry everything on. They all had short hair, tiny moustaches, shined boots, and called people their own age "Sir."

I wrote my first story. "Frontier City," of course. It felt very weird, writing about a battle in which I had just fought. I just couldn't do justice to the fear and despair, the aching that we had felt waiting for the assault to begin, wondering if we'd live out the night. And the fighting itself—words were no substitute for the real thing. The dichotomy between reality and the written word was simply too clear cut, and the emotional power of the experience too immediate. I was hit by a sort of writer's vertigo. It seemed as if my story was an act of betrayal in which truth, reality, and the men of my unit were sacrificed for the sake of false articulation.

After a few days of wandering around Tay Ninh, I began to feel like a dink who had deserted his outfit. When I read the story, I hardly recognized the battle and I knew it was no use. Horrible though it might be, I was hooked on reality. I packed my gear and returned to the field. What else was I going to do, become a combat soldier groupie?

I knew what I was asking for, heading back to Frontier City; but I had no choice. I thought about Kumo sitting on the bunker strumming his ukulele while we sang along and, though it might sound corny, it had been fun. About all I could look for if I stayed back in Tay Ninh was hanging out and getting drunk with the guys when they came back in for leave or R&R, and that wasn't my style.

Maybe it was that same kind of schoolboy mindset that got us through Basic and AIT that drove me back to Frontier City—that I'd-rather-be-dead-than-be-a-turkey kind of thing that gets kids to do all sorts of crazy things they should not do, like jumping off the tall ledges at the gorge or going back to a unit famous for self-extinction. And maybe it was something more.

I suppose you could call it love.

I guess I always knew that if I was going to be in the army, then I was going to be an infantryman. Once I'd been an infantryman, there was no way I could ever be anything else. That's just the way it is. I loved those bastards and, if they were going to die, I didn't want to hear about it back in Tay Ninh and spend the rest of my life with the images of Melvin and Pincush and Francis and the other guys haunting my dreams. I was going to die with them.

I hated the war and I wanted it to be over. I didn't want to have to return to Frontier City. I wanted to survive my tour and start a family. I wanted to have children and watch them grow, have crops to plant and a lawn to mow. But as long as my unit was there, I had no choice other than to go back.

I returned to the field with the full understanding that if we were hit again, the battle would be worse than the one at Mole City. I expected, as did most of the guys, that the second time around we would be wiped out. You can only be so lucky in war, and the NVA weren't that stupid.

Perhaps that was the attraction of Frontier City: a desire to experience the ultimate battle. I guess I had changed those last few months. I was in a death pact now. I really was in Suicide Charlie. We all were. We didn't know it. We never talked about wanting to die. We just did.

Sometimes, when the night moved with shapes and sounds made of memories, I fantasized about what it would have been like to be one of the Spartan soldiers at Thermopylae. As I envisioned the scene, everybody would be dead but me. The Persians would be pouring through the gap in the mountains and, as I stuck out my bloody short sword, I would shout, "Come on, you dirty bastards, eat me for dinner."

Then I'd never have to wonder, Are they coming again tonight?

——14——

"Dear John" Letters

The gritty spray from the field shower washes over me as the generator pops and snarls, sucking up sand and water from an abandoned well. Women and children from a nearby village laugh and shout, gawking at our naked bodies as cool water strips away the sweat and grime from another day's sweep.

Soap is a precious commodity to the people who live near Mole City II, and I can see one young woman watching me like a hawk, her eyes never leaving my bar of soap as I wash up. I set it down to rinse off and she dashes through the spray to grab it. I am too quick and snap it back from the metal tray that hangs from the shower pole.

The dejected maiden stands at the edge of the shower area, pouting, hands on hips, shaking her finger at me. Her bright sarong is soaked and clings to her body, so slender and firm. I set the soap back in the tray and, giggling like a little girl, she makes a second pass. This time, I reach out and grab her arm. She is a gentle thief, with her dancing brown eyes and teasing smile. I hold her for a moment, but she is strong, her arm is wet and slippery, and she pulls away, the bar of soap firmly in her grasp.

I don't mind. I'd trade a bar of soap for a smile any day.

We were all glad to get the hell out of Frontier City. Every night we wondered if this was the night they were coming again. The steady harassment from mortars and rockets that the enemy fired at us was a constant reminder that just across the border sat an enemy division, maybe two or three, and we were blocking their way. If they came back, they would be better prepared to blow us away.

The nightly terror had taken its toll. Sergeant Meredith decided to retire. Frontier City just sort of did him in. With twenty-seven years in the army, he knew he'd used up eight lives. Top, our first sergeant, a veteran of three wars who had won an Iron Cross as a boy fighting in the German Army during the Battle of Berlin, tossed in the banner also and moved into a bunker in Tay Ninh with Sergeant Meredith.

But no one was more relieved the morning in late May when we popped smoke and jumped choppers back to Tay Ninh for a three-day stand-down than Spec 4 Lopez. He was going home.

Lopez was a big Mexican who carried a radio for our platoon. He had extended his tour in Vietnam a month so that he could get out of the army as soon as he got back to San Francisco. Army policy was to immediately discharge enlisted men who DEROSed with less than 150 days remaining to serve. If we followed the straight shot through training and leave, the year in Vietnam cut our time remaining to 180 days. The temptation to extend to avoid chickenshit stateside duty was enticing, but Lopez was the only guy in Suicide Charlie who took the risk. He spent most of his last month at Frontier City. I guess that explains why it didn't happen often.

Lopez was one tough hombre, which I had learned a couple months earlier back at Mole City. Broad-shouldered and large-boned, he stood about six foot two in his bare feet. Though quiet and friendly by nature, he was from Texas and very sensitive about ethnic slurs.

We had installed a shower shortly before leaving the Mole, and one evening after sweep, somebody said to me, "Russell, call Lopez a 'wetback' and he'll punch you right in the mouth."

I didn't believe it. First of all, I considered us friends. Secondly, all those years in lily-white towns had still left me somewhat naive about the way prejudice could burn up a guy.

So I went up to Lopez while he was toweling down and, being a clever wise-guy type, I didn't just call him a wetback. I said, "Hey, Lopez, I bet all the towels in the world would never get your back dry."

He decked me. Laid me out but good with a firm right to the jaw. When I recovered my sensibilities, I tried to shake hands and apologize, but he wasn't interested. So much for anthropological inquiry on my part.

We weren't real close after that. Still, I was happy to see him go. Any guy who extended knowing he'd have to spend a couple more weeks on the border deserved an early discharge.

The rest of us had to settle for three days, with pay, back in Tay Ninh at a special area set aside for combat-weary outfits. Our holiday was called a stand-down: seventy-two hours of pot, booze, and barbecued chicken. Then it would be back to the bush to build a new base camp—Mole City II, this time—an above-ground version of the original because the rains would be coming later that summer.

Before he set us loose to party, Captain Pulliman gave us a good-going-guys-you-earned-it pep talk, telling us that we were the most highly decorated outfit in Vietnam. Nobody was much impressed, medals representing more of a curse than an honor. I don't know whether he got his numbers from Guinness or where but, given that a congenital coward such as myself had already been decorated twice for valor, there may have been some truth to his statement.

Stand-down was the end of the line for Captain Pulliman also. Line officers pulled six-month stints, unlike we enlisted grunts. Given their survival rates—about fifteen minutes in heavy combat—any company-grade officer who survived half a year in the field deserved a transfer to a more secure area, as well as a promotion.

I don't know if Pulliman made major out of Frontier City, which would have been a bit demeaning for the guy. He was a working man's officer not afraid to push a little dirt, crack a crease, or show some sweat under the armpits. He was the kind of guy you suspected wore suspenders when he was out of uniform.

Major is the most kiss-ass rank in the army and, based on his record, they should have bumped him straight to general. Instead they probably took him out behind some building and shot him. Guys like Pulliman who actually knew what they were doing must have been a threat to the paper-shuffling bureaucrats back in the Minister's office.

Once the captain was done with his talk, there was free beer on ice—Pabst, Miller, and Bud piled high and glittering in aluminum trash cans—mucho cigarettes to smoke (many discreetly packed with *kum sah*, Vietnamese for marijuana), a movie or two, and one Thai stripper, imported for the evening.

Who knows where they dug her up—the army moves in mysterious ways—but by sundown the word had gotten around and the stand-down area's flimsy covered grandstand was packed with one hundred lean, razor-eyed, borderline-psycho grunts who had not seen much female flesh for many many moons.

The stripper was short, squat, with a broad flat nose and thick lips: not exactly the exquisite features of a legendary Oriental beauty, but nobody was looking at her face. To the background of a scratchy copy of "The Stripper," she bumped and ground around the stage before an intensely appreciative audience. It didn't take her long to get down to the bare facts of her femininity, and then the real excitement began.

As she stripped, she tossed each item of clothing out to the wildly cheering throng. Some guys started tossing their clothes to her. She rubbed them against her crotch and threw them back into the sea of waving arms. Few were immune to the hysteria.

The fellow next to me, who had spent a couple months on the line before being shifted to company clerk, held a master's degree in history from Rutgers. Apparently, he too had answered question #39 wrong. Three times he tossed his aptly named bush hat onto the stage, receiving it back with glee each time and rubbing it against his face.

When the clothing exchange began to wear thin, one of the Kentucky or Indiana boys dropped down from the balcony and heaved himself prostrate on the stage, his tongue probing the air above his face. The stripper danced over and lowered herself onto his tongue. The idea caught on fast and soon one trooper after another tasted her buns until she was glazed over with sexual euphoria. Her pupils spread wide as an interstate highway as dozens of frenzied men crushed in toward the stage, eager for a taste. Thrusting out her arms, she shouted in a husky voice, "I just wish I could please you all."

That did it. The entire company rushed the stage. The officers who had hired her and were sitting in the front row raced before us, grabbing her by the arms and dragging her away to a chorus of boos and hisses.

Personally, I felt a little sorry for the stripper. Certainly, she meant what she had said and I doubt that she would ever again be admired so lustily.

As for the officers, I guess they got what they paid for.

The hootch girls and massage parlors must have been busy that night. The officers' careers were saved and tomorrow's headline did *not* read: "Foreign national raped to death by 100 drug-crazed American soldiers."

Talk about potential incidents.

Except for rare opportunities such as during our stand-down, infantrymen had to settle for sex with the boom-boom girls down at the barter point or go without. Horny as I was, as my Vietnam Sex Experience at New Mexico showed, I found it impossible to partake of their mercenary charms.

It wasn't just the idea of paying for it, though the lack of romance was a factor; but I also was disturbed by the fact that we were killing their men. Fucking the women, as well, struck me as fundamentally unjust.

It wasn't that way for everybody. One guy got the clap several times. He must have had a high tolerance for penicillin. He was a lanky six-foot carpet installer who boasted of laying bored housewives, as well as rugs. His own wife often wrote him lipstick-smeared letters composed as she lay in the bathtub. He was always reading between the water spots, so to speak, and claimed that he would kill her if he got home and found out that she had been playing around. No doubt he missed the irony of his attitude, and none of us was real quick to point it out to him.

"Dear John" letters were as common as flies on sores in Vietnam. Not many relationships seemed to last out the year. As Lucky once soliloquized during his brief stay in the outfit, if a woman found a dude with a longer dick and more money, she'd take him every time. I didn't share his cynicism, but mail call did leave a lot of guys with very long faces. Sometimes their loved ones didn't write to let them know it was quits.

A fellow in my platoon named Dave flew to Hawaii to meet his wife for R&R, and she never showed up. Didn't even bother to send a telegram saying tough luck, sucker. Just kept the money she had been receiving from her allotment of his pay and took the highway with some other guy, so he found out later.

Fortunately for Dave, he had struck up a conversation with a stewardess on the plane ride to Honolulu. She discovered him sitting, forlorn, in the hotel lobby the next day and took him in for the duration. Hers was a gesture of mercy that we all could appreciate.

Dave was not the only guy to get the sack. Basically, everyone with a girlfriend, fiancée, or wife eventually got one of those notes that started, "Dear . . . , This is very hard to say but . . ."

Everyone but the jealous carpet layer, that is. His wife stayed true right to the end. Chalk it up to the power of positive thinking.

I had received my "Dear John" back in Basic, but just before I shipped out for Vietnam Kelly rediscovered me. Lots of good drama in my situation, I figured, so I didn't take her newfound interest too seriously—even after a tearful last ride to the airport that day I shipped off and the frantic phone call she managed to get through to me in Oakland, when she asked me for a delay in my departure so that she could fly out and marry me. Based on past experiences, I had almost expected the eleventh-hour proposal, and I declined.

When my mail finally caught up with me in the field, the guys were amazed by the bulk of letters I received from her. I read them good humoredly and told everyone, just as I had in Basic, that it wouldn't last. But as the weeks rolled past, she kept writing. Page after page was filled with the minutia of her daily activities, and I read it all voraciously. Sometimes she would toss in some soft-porn fantasizing about what she was going to do when she finally got her hands on me again, and it was off to the ammo bunker for a visit with Five-fingered Mary. The ammo bunker was the only private spot in the base camp, for obvious reasons.

Six months of abstinence can make a twenty-year-old guy pretty horny, and as the time for my R&R rolled near I became very interested in taking Kelly up on her offer to meet me in Hawaii for a week of sun, surf, and sex. It was about the time we headed out from Tay Ninh after stand-down, choppering to a spot not that far from the original Mole City where we went to work building Mole City II.

The second Mole had all the extras: deluxe above-ground accommodations, a nice view of surrounding farmlands where we could watch local papa-sans tilling the fields with their wooden plows, and a shower some distance outside the wire where we went at the end of each day for a cool refreshing rinse.

Mama-sans lined the trail on the walk out, motioning for us to join them off to the side; but I wasn't interested. I did enjoy the way the younger ones would stroll along with us, joking and laughing, then pointing at us in mirthful ridicule when we stripped down and lathered up. Soap, as I had learned at New Mexico, was worth a roll in the elephant grass, so I didn't mind if they stole it, instead of selling themselves.

Mole City II was a mellow place. When Kelly sent a letter suggesting that maybe she shouldn't meet me for R&R after all, I didn't take it too hard. I figured I'd go somewhere else and have my fun. Then, out of the blue, she sent me a cassette tape recording. It was a spoken letter and, as I heard her voice for the first time in over half a year, she suddenly seemed real in a way that she—and America and my past, everything that came before Vietnam—had not seemed real for a long, long time. My heart ached with longing as, for a few minutes, I stepped out of the war and became eighteen again. I remembered my night in the bunker at Mole City and I knew that I had to see her one more time, just in case I didn't make it back to the States. So I sent her the money and told her to be there; then I started counting the days.

It wasn't often in Vietnam that we had something to look forward to. With the prospect of R&R coming closer, I began to relax a little. I was an experienced infantryman now, a veteran of two major battles and numerous smaller skirmishes. As a gunner, I usually stayed back when the company went out on sweep and, if I did go out, I knew a cold shower and a hot meal awaited me at the end of the day. Even in Vietnam, June was the kindest month.

It did not occur to me that my newfound sense of competence and well-being might be an indication of how much I had changed from those early days of terror and anxiety or that, in fact, I still felt much as I had when I first fell into the war—only now I was much better at submerging those feelings. In my mind, I still saw myself much as I was during my days back at the *Recorder*, and the thought of a plane ride straight from the war to the Real World, as we called the States, seemed perfectly natural. I was a civilian at heart, after all, and a soldier merely by chance.

When I met Kelly at Honolulu International, we embraced and kissed and did all the ritualistic reunion things that the mob of hysterical lovers around us did, but it was immediately apparent that something was missing. I felt stiff, awkward, almost formal as I took her arm and bags and led us toward a cab. When we reached our hotel, I felt oddly abstracted, surrounded as I was by gleaming porcelain, brightly painted walls, and white-washed stucco. After all those months of sleeping in the dirt, the mattress, the bed, the clean towels and folded linen seemed bizarre.

I had lost my license somewhere out in the bush, and Kelly was too young to rent a car, so we were stuck in downtown Honolulu near the Diamond Head. Honolulu was a tourist city, much like Florida. I wanted to go somewhere less crowded, but there was no way or time to get there so I tried to make the best of the situation.

The surf was piddling—worse than Indian Rocks Beach—but I rented a surfboard and made a game try of riding the midget choppers, to little avail. I got up once all afternoon. My values were in the right place, however. Man landed on the moon that week I was in Hawaii, but I went to the beach instead of watching it on TV. In just a few days I knew I'd be going back to a place far stranger than the moon.

One evening some young tourists had a beach party. They played guitars and sang "Ooh Bla Di Ooh Bla Da," a cheerful if somewhat nonsensical Beatles song. I found myself gradually edging closer to them, vicariously enjoying their carefree ambience. I wanted terribly to be included in their group but, of course, it was not possible. I was a stranger: a stranger to them, to Kelly, even to myself.

After a few days, I realized that Kelly was measuring me against someone else and I was coming up short. I couldn't relax, my jokes fell lame, my lovemaking was awkward. I couldn't help but feel a bit bitter after all the money I had spent when I could have gone to Hong Kong or Singapore and had a good time. I didn't understand that there was no way she could comprehend what I had been through over the last six or seven months. I didn't even understand it myself.

Our final day together we reached a silent understanding. She stopped judging me and I forgave her for being young, pretty, and free. When we returned to the airport, we did so with lighter hearts than we had felt all week. Just before I boarded the plane, she bought a postcard and had me sign it. I didn't notice who it was for; my thoughts were already far away.

Prisoners who break out of jail and are recaptured may understand how it felt to board that plane to fly back to the war. Chance left me sitting next to a remarkably empathetic air force colonel who spoke to me as if I were an equal. He told me that supply sergeants and black marketeers in Saigon were skimming off all the cream of the munitions heading toward the field while we grunts got the leftovers. They were eating prime rib while we gnawed on stringy beef. That did little to enhance my mood. Black marketeers were getting rich in Vietnam, and all we were doing was dying.

A few days later, I reached my unit at Mole City II, but it didn't seem like such a great place anymore. The June glow created by the anticipation of R&R was gone. After a couple weeks, Hawaii, Kelly, the rear, had all faded back into nonexistence. All I knew—had ever known, it seemed—was dirt, bunkers, C-rations, and bullets.

Then one day after we hiked back in from sweep I picked up my mail, and the clerk handed me something I couldn't quite place. It was a postcard from the guy in Hawaii who had signed it while waiting for the plane. His name was Norm Russell but it wasn't really me.

15

The Summer of '69

When Johnny comes marching home again,
hurrah, hurrah.
When Johnny comes marching home again,
hurrah, hurrah.

There is an old man in a hootch,
caught in the cross fire.
There is a boy in a bush
out on the border.
A lieutenant on the ground,
with a hole in his back.
There are 27 bodies inside the wire.

When Johnny comes marching home again,
hurrah, hurrah.
When Johnny comes marching home again,
hurrah, hurrah.

There is a girl at the dump,
run over by a truck.
A bunker, eight dead,
took a direct hit.
A soldier in Saigon,
who wanted to die.
There are 27 bodies inside the wire.

The women will cry,
the men will cheer.
And we'll all be dead,
we'll all be dead . . .

—*birthday poem, August 9, 1969. Age 21.*

There were about as many soldiers in Vietnam as there were hippies at Woodstock the summer of '69, and we camped out, too. When it rained we got muddy and swam naked in bomb crater pools. We smoked pot and sometimes hummed popular songs as we marched along, maybe picking a flower to stuff into the buttonhole of our fatigue jacket, and our hair was kind of long.

Out in the bush nobody gave you any shit, because you were carrying a rifle. In a firefight, you wanted to make damn sure the M-16s were all pointed in the right direction and that the guys on either side of you cared enough to cover your ass. Even a rebel like Sergeant Miller could ignore the rules as long as he didn't mind paying the price of being a frontline soldier right down to the very last days of his tour.

In a sense, we infantrymen were all rebels. We were the restless ones, the guys who were willing to take a chance. We were all draftees—USs, as Kumo had told that major back at the French Fort—whose service numbers began with US instead of RA, for regular army.

We were the guys doing most of the fighting. The army didn't expect much out of us as long as we were willing to squeeze the trigger.

Of the six hundred thousand men in-country when I was there, less than 20 percent were combat troops, the rest support. That's the way the American army operates. Takes a lot of swimming pool guards and chauffeurs to keep the boys in the field. That worked out to about 120,000 guys like me, swimming in the dust at Mole City II while the rest drove trucks, pushed paper, and did all the other things it takes to fight a war.

Interestingly, the NVA, with a fifty–fifty ratio of combat to support troops, maintained equivalent-sized fighting units despite having only half as many men in uniform in the South. That's what the army's own figures stated. Of the 8.5 million Vietnam-era vets, 2.5 million saw service in 'Nam. Twenty percent of that is 500,000. KIAs were about 50,000, wounded another 150,000. That's a 40 percent chance you wouldn't get through the war without at least picking up a piece or two of shrapnel, if you were infantry.

Out of a nation of 240 million people, we frontline grunts represented 0.0005 percent of the population. One in two thousand. Even among our own generation—the fabled "baby boomers"—we were a tiny minority. Vietnam infantry was definitely not mainstream. That was part of the attraction, I guess—the desire to do something different. Kind of made picking up a chunk of lead well worth the while.

After my failed R&R, I kind of lost touch with the so-called Real World. Kelly stopped writing but I didn't care. There were rock concerts and pennant chases back in the States but I was in the only place where reality intruded on a daily basis. My position had become fixed the moment I decided to bug out on Tay Ninh and return to Frontier City. R&R only made it clearer that I'd integrated the war into my own personal world view.

The first half of my tour had been pretty wild. With so much to learn, everything was new and my emotions had been a spinning kaleidoscope. Now I was a competent soldier, familiar with the routine, and I settled in for the duration. No longer reacting against the experience, I entered it and became part of it. A year is a very long time to a young man in a war and, after a while, I had to give in to Vietnam. Not that it would have mattered if I had continued to resist. Either way it was going to eat me alive.

Mole City II was not a bad place to spend the summer, what with the showers and the greenery. Things were a bit uncomfortable at first after Captain Pulliman left. His first replacement as CO was a captain shipped over from Battalion HQ. He was black, but color wasn't much of an issue in our outfit. Sure, some of the black dudes bitched from time to time about being discriminated against, but half of our leaders were black, or Hispanic, and the only thing that mattered was whether or not they could help us stay alive. A purple guy with warts on his head would have been fine with me if he could do the job.

The problem with that captain, however, was color as in OD, olive drab. The guy had lifer blood pumping through his veins. Cut him and it would have come out green. He did it by the numbers—and if the book said nobody outside without full combat gear when we were used to running around in T-shirts and boxer shorts, then into the fatigues we went, even if it was 110° in the shade.

Fortunately, he didn't last too long. Just punched his ticket and moved on. Short Round ran things for a while. He was Suicide Charlie all the way, and life smoothed back out into the easy glide.

Like I said, race and ethnicity weren't really issues in our outfit. I learned all I needed to know on the subject from Lopez, the time he decked me at the shower, and from an artillery NCO I knew in Tay Ninh. We were quaffing a brew at the enlisted men's club one day when I was passing through on my way back out to the field after R&R, and I brought up the subject, which had always confused me.

"I just don't quite understand prejudice," I told Jake, who was black and from Louisiana. "It always seemed to me that people are just people."

To back my case I told him about a night out at Mole City II when the unthinkable happened: the temperature dropped down into the 70s. I was freezing and didn't have a blanket or pancho liner, nothing but the slip-thin silk camouflage parachute cover that I used as my all-purpose wrap. None of the other guys had a cover to spare, and they were either too insensitive or too uptight to let me slide in with them. All except a new guy named Bob, a well-spoken black dude who waved me over and let me share his wool blanket, which he still had with him, being a recent arrival.

I'll always appreciate that simple gesture of kindness. To me it represented the way humans could step beyond barriers of race, social conditioning, and general self-centeredness and just be nice to one another.

Jake admitted my point in the specific incidence, but he wasn't buying the overall message.

"Let me just put it like this, Norm," he said, with a kind of long-suffering patience that I admired and aspired toward.

Jake was well into his late twenties, a true man of the world in my book, and I listened intently. He took a quick sip of his whiskey and turned in the stool to face me head on.

"There's some streets in New Orleans that I can't walk down the center of at high noon without a shotgun, and I'd still probably get blown away. And there's some other streets in that same city that you couldn't walk down at high noon without a shotgun, either. That's just the way it is."

Then he looked into my dumb naive eyes and just cackled.

"To think," he said, "that you are walking around here with an M-16 locked and loaded on full automatic and you still don't get it."

I guess that made his day.

There were a lot of things about Vietnam that I just didn't get without being hit in the face by them. One fine August afternoon we passed through a village and the local commander invited us into his HQ for a beer. He was young, an ARVN lieutenant who spoke excellent English, which was good, because none of us knew more than a few rudimentary words in Vietnamese, most of which had to do with sex or drugs. We chatted for a while, during the course of which I learned that he had recently returned from Fort Benning, where he had gone to helicopter flight school.

I was amazed. My old basic training site seemed like an infinitely more desirable locale than this border village in Tay Ninh Province. The beer was cold, a real treat. For the first time in a long time I was relaxing in a comfortable chair with a long cool drink and, without thinking, I blurted out, "Why did you ever come back to this?"

The lieutenant smiled patiently and shook his head.

"You Americans," he said. "You all think the world ends at the shore of the Pacific."

He gestured toward the glassless window of the yellow stucco building. Through the opening in the thick walls we could see fields that swept out from the village, where small brown people in pajamas and sarongs chopped at the ground with stout-handled hoes and an old man walked behind a wooden plow that was being pulled by a leather-harnessed water buffalo.

"These are my people," he said. "This is my land. I came back to fight for it, and them."

I never saw that lieutenant again. We did not get into the villages often. A few weeks later we did receive an intelligence report that some papers were found in an enemy cache indicating that his entire village was VC. When I learned that, I thought again about his words. He had only said whom he was fighting for, not whom he was fighting against. It could have been them, or us. Either way, I didn't like his odds.

The further I got into the war, the less sense it made. I had gone to Vietnam out of a sense of duty even though I was a pacifist by nature and did not believe wholeheartedly in this War, in specific. Once I'd gotten into combat, my emotions had taken over. Shock, horror, trauma, all rendered intellectual considerations impotent. The War had become an entirely personal matter. Early in my tour, mass graves had been discovered outside Hue. Thousands of people had been slaughtered by the North Vietnamese or Viet Cong when they took the city during the Tet Offensive in 1968. I saw the photographs of wailing mama-sans, the long rows of bodies that had been pulled out of shallow trenches, and they reinforced my *Reader's Digest* vision of the communists that I had gleaned from reading the missionary Dr. Tom Dooley's stories about the evacuation of the Vietnamese Catholics from the North after the defeat of the French by Ho Chi Minh's Viet Minh forces.

Then I shot the boy, heard the cry for his murder from my own men, learned of the ruthless way with which he had been dealt, and things didn't seem quite so clear anymore. New Mexico, the scene at the trash dump, Command's apparent callous disregard for the children, the way the villagers had to steal soap to be clean, as well as the story of the NVA soldier in the division magazine, all started to make me wonder. Why this war? Why would these people, these simple peasants, care who won?

Ho Chi Minh died while I was at Mole City II, and the South Vietnamese government declared it a national day of mourning. Once again, we weren't talking Einstein to figure out that something very strange was going on here. My feelings about the War, its justness and necessity, were not related to my feelings about the people who were caught up in it, however. They were an entirely different matter.

Once I realized that we were all conscripts—my comrades, the NVA, the villagers—who had been drafted into a war by somebody else who was sitting in an air-conditioned office somewhere in a plush chair behind a mile-deep desk, my attitude really changed. I knew who he was. I even had a name for him.

I figured the only way to get even with the son of a bitch was to get home safely. More and more my thoughts shifted away from the War as an abstract cause and toward concern for individual survival. I had a lot of life left to lead once I got back home. I didn't understand, couldn't understand, that the real world had been transformed within me. I had climbed that distant mountain, I had been to the top and seen the other side. My estrangement from America had become complete. It had now come to represent a mythic, totally impossible world—a concept, in fact, not so unlike Paradise.

Kumo had always talked of his dream for when he got home: to buy twin Vespa motor scooters for him and his girlfriend to drive while they attended Chico State College in California. I wondered if his dream had come true for him. Stan, I didn't know what his plans were. He was a floater. The kind of guy who would try a lot of things before he settled down. But I knew he would, someday.

Me? I was like Stan. A gunner and a good one.

Francis knew what he was going to do.

"I'm going to buy me a fucking whore," he told us one evening as we were sitting around the pit drinking beer, which was now allowed in the field since Williamson had been replaced by some other jerk as our Division Commander, "and fuck her with her panties on. Then I'm gonna' frame those panties, hang 'em on the fucking wall, and put a little sign over them that says, 'Vietnam, eat shit.'"

Everyone agreed he had the right idea.

Another new guy joined our squad that summer. He wasn't an FNG; he was a rifleman who was transferred over from one of the leg platoons. His name was Mike Leggitt and his hometown was easy to remember: Battleground, Washington.

Mike was one of the new kind of trooper that was starting to show up as the war dragged on—a college grad whose deferment had expired before the war did. Mike held a degree in English and we talked a lot about books and such. He knew lots of hundred-dollar words and would have had no problem with Same-same. He reminded me of Ron Runyon, the college grad I had known in Basic. He seemed to understand the war and the army in a way in which I could only catch a glimpse. With his pale blue eyes, thinning blond hair, and light skin, he appeared almost translucent, as if part of him was there, with us, and the rest somewhere else. I envied him his detachment that made him seem as if he was just passing through—which, in a sense, we all were, only he seemed to understand that better than the rest of us. He was a nice guy, but that degree still set him apart from most of the other enlisted guys. After a while he got a new job, driving a jeep for a general back in Tay Ninh. The officers liked someone behind the wheel to whom they could talk.

During the time he was with us, however, we learned what it had been like back on campus while we were in the army.

"You guys are fighting for yourselves," Mike told us. "Nobody back home cares about winning the War. They just want it over like Nixon promised it would be."

"What do you think's going to happen," Pincush asked. I could see pictures of home flashing in his eyes.

"Nothing. They'll just bullshit around until things quiet down, the protests ease off, then they'll escalate it some more. Nixon doesn't want to lose to the commies. He's the original master commiebaiter."

Not long after Mike joined us, rumors of a possible truce filtered down from Command. All we had to do for the time being was hold territory, they said, so that we could claim control of it when lines were drawn at the peace talks. It sounded good to me. Too good. I wasn't motivated like that ARVN lieutenant was. Somewhere over the course of the summer, I lost my will to fight.

We had a dog who walked point for us. His name was Spit, as in "spit in your eye." We called him that because he was such a tough little guy. He was a tan short-haired mongrel who had adopted Charlie Company somewhere along the way. He was a natural point dog, always staying about fifty feet to the front of the file whenever we were on sweep. When he smelled gook he went nuts. He also had a lock on a first ballot election to the Vietnam Hall of Fame, along with Rocko, Lopez, Sergeants Miller and Meredith.

As most dogs over there seemed to, he hated the locals with a passion and loved Americans to a proportionate degree. His animosity toward the

Vietnamese came naturally: they ate dog. He had been with us for most of my tour, hanging loose, eating real good, and generally appreciating not having to worry about ending up in some villager's stew pot. Over the months I had grown quite fond of him.

One afternoon, as my company was moving through an open field, he disappeared into a tree line and went berserk. A rifle squad moved up slowly to check out the ruckus but, before they got there, the NVA troops lying in ambush lost their cool and took Spit out with a burst of gunfire. End of dog. End of ambush.

They were dug in deep and could have hurt my unit real bad if Spit hadn't smelled them out. Instead, Suicide Charlie took them out with a classic frontal assault, walking straight in over the top.

I was back at the gun when it happened. Some of the guys grabbed their gear and headed for the chopper pad when they got the word. I didn't go with them. It's not that I was afraid. It was just that I did not care. I knew that I should, but something inside of me had broken and I hadn't figured out how to fix it yet.

When I heard the news about Spit, I felt real bad. I guess, right about then, I could relate to a dog better than I could to a human. He had his reasons for how he felt, and they were not reproachable. He was a lot like the lieutenant who had given me the beer. They were both willing to die for a cause that they cared deeply about. We were killing the so-called enemy just because they were there.

Later I felt great shame for my dispassionate response but, at the time, I simply didn't give a shit. Why didn't they just turn around and walk back out of there, I wondered, and leave those poor bastards alone.

One afternoon I was hanging loose by my gun and watching an old papa-san plowing his field when a chopper landed at the pad outside the bunker line. An FNG hopped out, a lieutenant with one of those silly little bars on his lapel. He trotted in all breathless and hurried over to me.

"He shouldn't be out there, should he?" the lieutenant asked.

I couldn't answer right off, I was choking too hard on my laughter, but I figured I'd better say something before he ran out and shot the guy with his .45.

"Why not, it's his field," I said. "He's been plowing that field since sunrise, he'll be plowing it till sundown. He's probably been plowing that field for ten thousand years."

The lieutenant looked at me through wide eyes, as if he'd seen some kind of oracle.

"Ten thousand years," he said. "Did you say ten thousand years?"

"That's right," I replied. "I'd say he's about half done."

I don't know what happened to that lieutenant, but he looked like the kind that would benefit from a quick trip back to Philadelphia. They must have been running a little short on officer stock by then because we got one eventually, near the end of my tour, and he was a real beaut.

That night, or another not long after, I was sitting in my bunker engaging in my, our, everybody's favorite activity—checking out my short-timer's calendar. By then, the pages were faded and worn. It had a lot of Xs on it, one for each day in-country. As I looked back over the months, each holding memories, it occurred to me that I'd been in Vietnam a long, long time.

I picked up my pencil to scratch out another day. One more gone, if I made it through the night. After I made my mark, I flipped the pages back all the way to December and looked at those first scraggly Xs. How huge and distant the year had seemed to me then, at the original Mole City. I had counted on Kumo and Stan during those early days. They had seemed so wise.

Then it hit me. They had understood what I was just starting to figure out. They never talked about the commies or killing Cong. They grumbled about Command and spoke softly about friends who had died. And when the enemy attacked, they fought with fierce cold efficiency. They understood their mission in simple direct terms: to stay alive, and keep us alive also.

Slowly, I leafed through the remaining pages of my calendar. Less than ninety days to go. I touched each one with my finger. I can make it, I said to myself. I looked around the bunker. In the muted glow of the flashlight I could see Francis and Pincush, Melvin, Mike, and Bob sleeping there.

Vietnam, eat shit, I thought, remembering Francis's words. When I get home I'm going to hang this calendar on the wall so I can look at it every day and remember how lucky I am to be back in America. I flicked off my flashlight and stretched out on the ground. When I closed my eyes I could see a picture of myself back in AIT, marching out to the rifle range chanting "When Johnny Comes Marching Home Again."

How that chant had spooked me at the time. We had been trained from the very beginning to accept the inevitability of our deaths, and I had bought right in. Fatalism was the source of our courage. Otherwise we wouldn't be crazy enough to expose ourselves enough to return fire. We'd end up like those NVA that my company had walked right in on, cringing out of fear.

Ever since that night at Mole City I had been locked in a death trance, but now—for the first time since we'd been overrun—I didn't want to die. It was a horrible, horrible feeling, to be trapped in Vietnam and to care about staying alive. If I was determined to live, I would need to find the strength to face death somewhere. And I knew where to look for it. It was right there, right inside my bunker.

We are all going to make it, I vowed. We owe it to each other.

16

Apparitions

The sappers are wraiths who come in the night. I can't see them, can't hear them. I can only think them and, in my mind, they are always here.

The night moves in small pieces. As I stare into the dark, things appear to creep up to my bunker. My eyes do not adjust smoothly to changes in the light. They click abruptly from one f-stop to another, adjusting in jumps that jerk everything a few paces closer. Bushes, trees, tufts of grass all seem to be slowly working their way in toward the perimeter until I am confronted by an army of vegetation.

It is difficult to tell the difference between plants and people, sleep and consciousness, the fantastic and the real. All certainty has vanished.

Hour after hour, the sappers inch through the hypersensitive concertina wire with its taut ganglia of flares and mines, working their way in, closer and closer. Passage through it seems impossible—and yet suddenly they are upon us, swarming through the basecamp like locusts, clicking and buzzing with death.

In March, when word came down that we might be headed for the French Fort, the veterans did not like it at all. They shook their heads and stared to the east, as if looking for something that was invisible to us. Their jaws clenched; a mutinous glint sparked from their eyes.

We went, of course, rotating through on our way to Delta, staying just long enough for us new guys to get a taste of the place. Long enough to understand why the veterans felt the way they did about it. Long enough that when orders came to Mole City II for us to pack our gear and prepare to rotate back there, I reacted just as had Kumo, Stan, and the other guys so many months before.

The base was not a fort at all, at least not in the sense those of us who had grown up on John Wayne and F Troop thought of one. There was no gate, no stockade or courtyard, just a dirt berm pushed up by bulldozers, a permanent bunker line, and a massive battery of artillery pieces that roared throughout the night. It was a grim, dirty, shadeless place where you baked all day in the hot sun. It also had an excellent view of Nui Ba Den, where Short Round had tried to send me from New Mexico and where the sappers hung out when they weren't sneaking through the wire.

It did have a few redeeming aspects. An honest-to-goodness mess hall, the kind with tables, chairs, and a roof. Hot meals every sundown. Nonreconstituted scrambled eggs for breakfast. But they were all part of the illusion, because what the French Fort actually was was a target.

The base had been around for so long that the enemy had a complete fix on it. Night after night we were blasted with devastatingly accurate mortar fire. I eventually decided that papa-sans trained their grandchildren in the art of shelling Americans there. They would trot out the old 60mm pocket mortar—a gun so small it could be fired from the thigh the way John Wayne always did his fifty-calibre machine gun—then set it up under the same tree the old man had carved his initials in when he was a boy, and sight in on the fort. I could almost hear them talking.

"Just to the right of that twig, there, junior, and boom, there goes the mess hall. Over to left, second branch from the top, and, pow, there goes third squad's mortar pit." (That's me!)

Making allowances for new growth, they must have carried on for generations, passing on the tube, so to speak. It was an insomniac's delight. Can't sleep tonight, or just feeling antsy, then go out and bloop a few into the fort. Make those American boys sweat a little. Make 'em earn their $67-a-month hazardous duty pay. Then, for good measure, toss in a few sappers.

There was twenty years of wire outside the French Fort. Row after row of giant Slinkys made from tangled concertina wire edged with razor blades encircled the base. Strewn through the loops of steel were countless trip wires that triggered flares, booby-traps, mines, even tin cans filled with pebbles. To me, it was a seemingly impassable barrier even in the daytime, yet night after night the sappers passed through that barricade like fish through water.

There is a boundary in the mind where thought passes from the conscious into the unconscious. The sappers passed through that boundary as well.

During World War II, Japanese soldiers supposedly would sneak up on American foxholes where two men were sleeping and slit the throat of just one, leaving the other to wake up and find his buddy dead. It was the psychological equivalent of shooting for the legs. The wounded require assistance. They hamper a unit more than the dead do.

The North Vietnamese were masters of the art of psychological warfare. They knew that, even if they couldn't beat us on the battlefield, they could beat us in our hearts and minds.

Wounds of the mind are different from wounds of the body. They are harder to recognize, harder to treat, harder to recover from, and they are not borne with pride. The army does not give purple hearts for psychic wounds, though perhaps it should. That might remove the stigma from psychological casualties and help them recover. Amputees often experience referred pain—the agony of loss remaining in the mind although the limb is gone. Just as physical wounds can lead to psychic pain, wounds of the mind can create physical symptoms. These are called "conversion reactions."

Sometimes when people are dealing with things so elemental as dark and light, good and evil, weak and strong, they forget how subtle the mind is. The North Vietnamese never did. They trained regiments of sappers and sent them to the South to haunt American soldiers who had one overriding goal: to survive their 365 days of madness and return to sanity. It was a war of the fanatic against the pragmatic, the mad Mythic East against the rational Real World, and it was not an even contest.

The sappers truly were wraiths, apparitions of living men visible just before death. They were suicide soldiers who were trained to die. Once they entered the wire, they would be executed if they came back out again without proof that they had infiltrated the base camp.

Sometime in early September I reached the most dangerous point in my tour, the final ninety days. I had survived the summer of '69, as well as the spring and the winter, and what had once seemed a vast uncrossable distance of time—a whole year—had shrunk to a small clustering of months. The realization of my shortness had snapped me out of my death trance and, now that I wanted to live, I was more vulnerable to the terror and disorientation of the war. It was just then that we returned to the fort.

At the French Fort, the sappers and the mortar fire combined to fuck with everybody's mind. I knew that from our first trip through, but it was much worse the second time around. After more than nine months in-country, my nerves were starting to unravel and things got real loose.

We'd be out in the pit returning fire, concentrating on trying to knock out the enemy gunners, and sappers would pop up atop the bunkerline, shooting at us to drive us away from our guns. Guys on bunker guard would snap alert as a shape charge was being stuffed into their gun port, or a bayonet into their belly. It was a vicious type of combat that tested our minds more than our bodies, and all those months of ignoring enemy fire had taken its toll on me.

One afternoon as I lay in my bunker grabbing some shuteye before another long night, I felt someone tapping me on the shoulder. I looked up, my eyes following the line of the hand and arm that reached in through my mosquito net. Just past the split in the transparent mesh, the arm ended. It dissolved into space. I was wide awake and looking at a hand, arm, and nothing more. It dissolved into shredded flesh, like that of the dead bodies I had dragged to the mass grave. Shaken, I staggered out into the sunlight, but even the clarity of midday no longer provided relief from anxiety.

About that time, I started sensing incoming when there was none. I would be sitting by the pit, talking to Pincush or Mike Leggitt, and the certainty would grip me that a round was dropping on us. I knew I could always hear the screech of rockets and the oomph-oomph of mortars long before impact. They were sounds to which I responded instinctively. I was perfectly safe and yet I felt compelled to dash into our bunker, believing that, if I did not move immediately, a mortar would hit us right where we were sitting.

Whenever this compulsion overcame me, I would ease toward the bunker, slowly at first, then faster and faster as my mind filled with the image of a descending round, until panic at last chased me racing the final few steps. Diving inside, I would breathlessly await the explosion. But none ever came. I would go back outside feeling pretty foolish, but nobody said much about it. I wasn't the only guy ducking imaginary rounds.

Those mad dashes to the bunker were the first clear signs that my mind was starting to go. What they meant was that I was starting to believe I was the one who made things happen, when actually they were totally out of my control. Reality had become too powerful for me, and I was now experimenting at creating my own. But my version was a disjointed and chaotic reality, nonetheless, because it incorporated so much of what really did exist there in Vietnam.

The 60mm mortars, for example, were small, but the damage those goose-egg-sized rounds could do was amazing. One night the main ammo bunker took a direct hit. My gun pit was right next to it. I was out returning fire when the ammo dump blew and the world erupted in a Karakatoa-class explosion. Thousands of artillery rounds and black powder charges exploded simultaneously. Fortunately, there was a ten-foot-high dirt berm around the dump or I would have been vaporized instantly. Due to the wall, the explosion went off like a massive volcanic-shape charge.

At the sound of the blast, I instinctively hit the ground. I looked up to see a sky on fire. Flames were descending on me in a slow voluptuous arc. I was only a few feet from my bunker and low-crawling at a record rate but, like the night I outleaped the rocket splash at Frontier City, time seemed to stand still. With one eye skyward on the falling fireball, it took forever to cover that short distance. Time passed as in one of those interminable nightmares where one tries to dodge an oncoming automobile or reach a ringing telephone and never seem to quite get there. When I did reach the bunker, sweat was weeping from my body and my lungs were as tight as those of a marathoner charging up Heartbreak Hill in Boston.

Melvin was up in the tower and he radioed for every medi-vac chopper in the Division. Miraculously, only a few men were hurt badly. The explosion was so massive it blew right up and out of the base camp. Beams as big as railroad ties were found far beyond the wire. All that was left of the ammo dump was a smoking crater. Any unit depending on fire support from the French Fort that night was out of luck.

After the ammo blew, things got very grim. The following night I was ordered to fire on children who hung out at the trash dump. Command claimed that FOs were sneaking in with them and staying there after dark to direct incoming fire.

My initial reaction was to refuse, as anybody who'd been at New Mexico with me would have anticipated. Then I asked them what they would do instead. Order someone else to fire, was the reply. So I reconsidered. I knew I was a damn good gunner and I could count on myself to miss. I wasn't so certain about the other two gunners in my platoon.

I believe I fired well that evening. They didn't bring any kids in for treatment at the aid station the next morning and we didn't find any five year olds decomposing in the dawn. The entire episode did little for my attitude, however. War, I was beginning to understand, is a no-win situation.

The army maybe had tricked me again. It had dropped me into a pit of madness, plundered my soul, and soon it was going to ship my burnt-out husk back to the States, dead or alive, but I was not going back with any more dead children on my conscience.

At this point, the War became one of two fronts. There was the enemy Out There and the enemy Inside. I had begun my War Year with a notion of the enemy soldiers as apparitions because I had never seen them. They weren't real for me before the night of the first attack. Now I knew the enemy relatively well. I had shot at them and been shot at by them in turn, had touched them, both alive and dead, for we had taken some prisoners. I had, in the case of the boy, even felt their pain. Despite all of that, I once again began to perceive them as apparitional. It didn't make any difference that rational thought argued forcefully that the sappers were real human beings made of flesh and blood, cells and molecules. They spoke to a deeper seat of knowledge. The one where we differentiate between good and evil.

I know we killed some, but I never saw their bodies. To me it seemed that, when they died they just disintegrated as if they were creations of our imaginations. They were like smoke, we were like smoke, our guns made smoke against the darkness and they disappeared into it.

But they were not the only internal enemy with which I had to deal. At some point, all of life is myth, all reality is subjective. Usually we live inside that myth and we never experience the subjective as the interstitial emotional tissue that it is, the stuff that binds that myth together. At the French Fort, I began to experience the collapse of reality as part of the process of creating a new one—one in which it might be possible to explain the death of the boy, the misery of the children at the refuse piles, the coldness of leaders who could call in fire on them. The sappers were the perfect point of entry for a journey into a new world. They seemed to materialize as if on a whim, then vaporize just as capriciously. All they needed were black hoods and eyes that glowed in the dark like red coals and I could have recognized them for what they really were. That would have made my life so much easier.

One afternoon when I was sitting in the bunker waiting out a couple imaginary rounds, I told Leggitt about the apparition I had seen. He didn't seem particularly surprised.

" 'Then glided out of the joyous wood, the ghastly wraith of one that I know,' " he said, quoting Tennyson.

" 'His presence scared the clan, who held him for some fleeting wraith, and not a man of blood and breath,' " he continued, shifting to Scott. "Not anyone you recognized, I hope," he added. "Say, me, for instance."

That's what I liked about Leggitt. He kept things in perspective.

"Now that you mention it," I said, taking a closer look at his sleeve, "there was a certain similarity."

"Aha," he responded. "Then it must have been someone else. I just put this on. I'm on my way out the door. Got myself a job driving a jeep for some stuffed shirt with a star."

He picked up his duffel bag with a jerk and tossed the strap across his shoulder.

"Think it's safe out there right now?" he added with a wink. "I'd hate to arrive as a puddle of ectoplasm. General might not like that."

"Safe enough," I said, thinking how his presence would be missed by me and thinking about how he was a little bit like an apparition himself, with his pale complexion and wandering ways. "But I wouldn't count myself safe for certain until I was in the chopper and around the mountain."

"Around and down," Leggitt agreed. "Two feet on the ground."

He tapped me on the shoulder and headed out the entrance.

"I'll be seeing you soon enough. Make sure you say hello on your way through to Hong Kong. Hanging out with generals ain't exactly my favorite pastime, you know. But it sure beats Saturday nights with sappers."

Then, like Stan and Kumo and so many other guys before him, he disappeared.

With Leggitt gone, I felt even more isolated than I had before. He had added a certain air of bemusement to the French Fort experience and the War in general that no one else seemed able to provide. Phil had left months before, and Leggitt was the first guy to come along who could really replace him in the philosophic department. Pincush lacked the romantic aspect. Francis? Forget it. Melvin was a closet lifer soon to be shifted to FDC. Without Leggitt to bounce some of my ideas off of, my thoughts shifted more and more inside.

The one thing that made my situation the most bearable—the fact that I was nearing the end of my tour—was somewhat of a double-edged sword. As an official short-timer I had unconsciously begun the process of emotional withdrawal that preparing to leave my unit required. Unlike someone such as Mike, I wasn't very good at it, as my earlier attempts at separation demonstrated. The truth was, I needed the army more than the army needed me. But I didn't know it and neither did they. Or if they did, they didn't care.

I still thought that when my 365 days were over, I would be able to turn my back and walk away. Unfortunately, as Ulysses had learned four thousand years before, I was soon to find out that departing the battleground marks the beginning of a journey on treacherous waters. I was entering into a spiritual conflict against an ancient enemy compared with whom the sappers were merely apostates.

I had climbed that narrow staircase after all, and I was standing before the door. But I didn't want to open it because I feared that the man in the attic might be me.

─── 17 ───

Songs

My fatigues are threadbare and wrinkled, a soldier's cross dangles from my faded bush hat, my boots have yet to see polish, and my hair pushes out from my collar. I am a survivor of Suicide Charlie who has long since passed over the thin red line that separates combat soldiers from normal men.

I have come straight from the field and made a quick journey from Tay Ninh to a holding area outside of Ton Son Nhut Air Base, where I am waiting for my flight to Hong Kong. Ten months in-country and this is my reward: seven-day leave from the war. I am standing outside a small cabin where we are to spend the night. A major walks up and starts giving me shit about my hair and my appearance in general.

"I think you'd better clean up, Sergeant," he barks, staring me hard in the face. "Get yourself some fresh clothes and a haircut or you won't ship out. That's an order."

I don't salute the major, his words barely register, and I don't bother to answer him. I just look through him with my personal version of the thousand-meter stare and, after a bit, he wilts, fades into the twilight, and disappears.

I don't know if he vaporizes. I don't even notice him leave. It just gets dark after a while and I go inside because only a fool would stand outside at night in Vietnam without a rifle in his hands.

The newspaper correspondents described Vietnam as the first rock'n'roll war. A catchy phrase but definitely untrue. The war was country'n' western.

I was in an NCO club in Cu Chi while passing through on my way to

Hong Kong and they had a Filipino C&W band—little guys in tall Stetsons, sequins, cowboy boots, the whole bit. The lead singer was about five foot two, 110 pounds, and he was grunting out "Ring of Fire" in a perfect imitation of gravel-voiced Johnny Cash.

Government-sanctioned entertainment. The army must have felt that country'n'western was good for the war effort, because they played it all day long on Radio Vietnam. Country boys like Francis all had fat Japanese PX radios with built-in tape recorders. They would tape all day, then play it back again at night. There was no escape.

During the days that I stayed back at the patrol base there wasn't much else to do but listen to the radio. I learned to hate Gene Weed. One might think that a guy with a name like Weed would be into psychedelic rock'n'roll—a little Quicksilver Messenger Service, Cream, the Moody Blues. Forget it. Weed was on every morning spinning "God Don't Make Little Green Apples" by O. C. Smith. Thought it was the greatest piece since Beethoven's Fifth.

In between songs he interviewed so-called starlets.

"Hey guys, get a load of her wheels" (wheels meaning legs), he would urge us from his studio in Saigon or Burbank or wherever the hell was the box they kept the guy in when he was carrying on space-brained dialogues with out-of-work refugees from *Return of Beach Blanket Bingo*. I could only sit in my gun pit and marvel. Who in the world came up with Gene Weed. Some ironic s.o.b., no doubt, sent straight from the Ministry of Misery.

We rock'n'roll fans had only one show and it came on at about 10 P.M. The intro was classic fifties schmaltz: "Come fly with me, get high with me, go halfway to the moon." I figured it was the only way the announcer could get past the censors. That was our show—the same ironic bastard back in Saigon playing Perry Como singing about getting high.

I wonder what he was smoking.

Nighttime was a good time to light up, but I didn't smoke marijuana much. It made me paranoid and I was already nervous enough. Early in my tour I bought some once from a small boy at the barter point. He sold me a bulging paper sack full of Cambodian Red for two dolla' MPC. A strange experience, copping from a kid, but it was righteous weed.

Now and again at Mole City I, I might find myself in a bunker full of like-minded individuals and we would smoke a number. Papers were hard to come by, so we'd knock the tobacco out of a cigarette and fill it with *kum sah*. I always enjoyed watching the southern country boys like Francis turn on for the first time. Marijuana can be like a religious experience when you first get into it, and they were quick to become believers.

Pot smokers had a common fantasy: An American and an NVA soldier meet in the jungle. Neither has the drop on the other, so they put down their rifles, pull out a bag of pot, and smoke a jay.

Maybe it really did happen. In this crazy war, anything was possible. I could easily imagine the enemy soldiers sitting around their campfires listening to Radio Vietnam and cursing the damn country and western.

One thing we knew for certain was that the NVA was into junk. Sometimes we found bags of the stuff on dead assault troops. Stone 'em up before they hit the wire. One guy with a bit of a medical background claimed that heroin did something to the blood to make it coagulate faster in case of a wound, but I don't think that was the real reason they took the stuff. Try to envision assaulting a typical American patrol base. Talk about firepower. I would have to be hopped up to even think about it.

But, for the NVA, that was their business. They had to be aware of the likelihood that they would be shredded by lead, and they dealt with the possibility in what, by American standards, was an almost unimaginable way. The enemy soldiers dug mass graves before they attacked us so they could quickly hide the bodies afterward. Now that's real commitment. And they wore bandanas around their necks to make it easier to drag their bodies back to the border. The NVA understood body count.

Digging their own graves must have been standard procedure for the sappers who hit us at the French Fort. In fact, after three weeks of waiting and wondering if this was the night I was going to get mine, I was about ready to pick up a shovel and start digging, myself, just to get it over with.

Near the end of that second stay at the fort we got a new CO. He was an ex–Green Beret captain who'd switched to the regular army so he could make rank. As part of the arrangement, he had been promised command of Suicide Charlie. We were a demand item on the officer's advancement ladder.

He wanted us but we were not so sure that we wanted him. Promotion-hungry gung-ho officers are the kind that can get you killed in a hurry. He did, however, promise to get us out of the French Fort pronto and back into the bush. He didn't care much for patrol bases, he said, preferring to roam the jungle.

His plan was that we would start pulling "bushmasters," extended stays in the field during which we would hide by day and move at night, setting up ambushes in hopes of catching off guard the NVA troops infiltrating across the Cambodian border. These tactics were a reflection of those devised by our new division commander, Major General Harris Hollis, who replaced Williamson in September. Hollis had emphasized small-unit operations when he commanded the 9th Division down in the Mekong Delta and, now that we'd knocked the shit out of the NVA main force units, he decided we had to go out after them and initiate the contact ourselves.

Theory was that the enemy wasn't accustomed to American troops setting up night ambushes so close to their sanctuaries. That, after all, was more down their alley. It struck me as risky business: They were closer to reinforcements than we were and, if we hit a battalion or regiment, we could be in deep shit and probably dead long before sunrise. That possibility aside, the thought of ditty moiing the French Fort struck a responsive chord in me.

After ducking all those imaginary rounds, I was ready for a change of scene. It was close to my time for leave, clean sheets, restaurant food, and no rats scurrying across my chest at night; and the waiting was getting on my nerves.

To replace Mike, we picked up a new squad mate named Ray who, like Leggitt, was a refugee from a rifle platoon. Ray was a rowdy, boisterous short-timer just back from leave and still feeling the glow of good times. He had gone to Australia, and the Land Down Under had done right by him. Australian men, he explained, did not pay much attention to women, so the gals waited at the airport and nabbed horny GIs right off the tarmac. A tall blue-eyed blond-haired lovely had stole him off to the mountains where they spent his week drinking wine and fucking under the stars. Sydney sounded good to me but I already had tickets for Hong Kong and it was too late to change the order.

Our last night at the fort, we celebrated our imminent departure by going on rat patrol. The place swarmed with big ones and they ranked only slightly behind the sappers and incoming in terms of annoyance. The moon was bright that night as we waited outside our bunkers armed with shovels and clubs, and dressed in just steel pots, combat boots, and boxer shorts. One fellow ran in and banged the hell out of a garbage can lid. As the rats fled, we swooped down on them, flailing away and chasing them all over the base camp. We didn't get many—they were quick—but it was the chase that counted. I guess they were paying for our weeks of tension from fighting an invisible enemy. Regardless, it was great sport. With all the racket we were raising, the sappers weren't coming in that night. They must have thought we could chase their spirits right back out into the night.

After rat patrol, the artillery kicked in with a good-bye serenade. Ray hopped up on the bunker with a bayonet for a baton and played conductor to the percussion section of the American Artillery Orchestra. Leonard Bernstein in skivvies and a steel pot, flicking back imaginary coattails. He anticipated the firing nicely. With a wave of his baton, bam, bam, bam, off went a battery of 155s. A slow sweep of his arm, punctuated with subtle wrist snaps, summoned the staccato rat-tat-tat-rat-tat-tat of the little 105s while the air still rumbled from the mighty blasts of the 175s. A giant arc with both of his arms raised high over his head called forth the resounding eight-inchers, ker-boom, ker-boom, a fitting climax to the combat sonata. All the piece lacked was a counterpoint of enemy mortars and a coda of small-arms fire. Not that we were terribly disappointed by their lack. They were not music to our ears.

The next morning we loaded up and headed for the chopper pad. I knew I would never see the French Fort again, but I was not feeling nostalgic. Night ambush may not have struck me as an ideal short-timer activity, but it was eminently preferable to life inside the bull's-eye of a target on the Vietnam artillery range. After spending so much of my tour in patrol bases, I was looking forward to staying out in the field. I thought it would help make time pass faster, and it did. I quickly fell into the rhythm and flow of days and nights uninterrupted by base camp details that constantly called attention to the passing of the hours.

The monsoon season had arrived, and the sky would cloud over at dusk. We would set out our claymore mines and take our positions, sitting in the October dark, waiting and watching for enemy soldiers. Wrapped in my thin slip of silk, the warm steady rain beating down on me, I slipped into a world without time. For ten months I had lived and dreamed for the day I would become a short-timer—and now that I was one, my thoughts kept drifting toward the past, perhaps just to help ease my anticipation.

Night ambush is an intensely personal experience. Some nights the dark was so deep, the air so thick, that I might have been inside a sensory deprivation tank.

As I waited for the enemy to appear, songs kept floating into my consciousness, calling forth memories such as the morning I flew off to Oakland to leave for the war. I was gliding down the runway at Bradley Field as Kelly waved from the observation deck. I slipped on the headphones and waved back. She was just a tiny figure in black with her arm stretched high in the air while Simon and Garfunkel sang "Are you going to Scarborough Fair? Parsley, sage, rosemary, and thyme. Remember me to one who lives there. She once was a true love of mine." My heart filled with aching sadness and I had answered back silently, No, I'm going to Vietnam.

A few months earlier I had been sitting in the barracks at Fort McClellan shining my boots that first night of AIT after receiving my infantry assignment and the old Negro spiritual "Michael, Row the Boat Ashore" was cycling through my head. It seemed so appropriate. A World War II veteran once told me that being in the army was like being a slave and, as I remembered the words "The River Jordan's deep and wide, alleluia. Milk and honey on the other side, alleluia," I could almost feel the pull of the oars and hear the quiet lapping of the water against the hull. Sitting out on ambush, I realized at last where freedom lay. I could feel the tide, the flow of my life passing through space and time as if it, also, was made of water and my body a small vessel that I worked against the current until I reached the other side of the dark river that Ulysses called Styx.

I recalled how in AIT we used to chant as we marched that we would all be dead by the summer of '69 and I wondered if, in some small secretive way, we were not anxious for death, having been living in its presence for so long. After having crossed the dark river so many times in our dreams and fears, it got damned difficult to keep returning to the nearer shore. Death, I began to realize, has an allurement, a fascination that is hard to shake once you have been close to it. Suicide started to make sense. It was just another option in a set of possible responses. Weren't we all supposed to be dead already?

The opposite of death was DEROS, end of tour, Homeward Bound. The song that conveyed all the hopes and dreams of us infantrymen was Scott MacKenzie's "If You're Going to San Francisco." Planeloads of hardened veterans were said to burst into tears upon hearing that ballad over the intercom near the end of their flight home. Not that everybody got treated so well when they got back, what with demonstrators throwing rocks and spitting at the disembarking GIs. But it was the thought that counted: "Be sure to wear some flowers in your hair. . . . You'll meet some gentle people there."

Maybe if the hippies had been more broadminded they would have understood that we weren't so different. If anything, we wanted peace a lot more than they did. And we sure as hell were anxious to get to San Francisco.

My final flight was less than two months away when my leave orders came down. Word caught up with us somewhere along the border, and I eagerly hopped the next resupply chopper into Tay Ninh. The only sad part about leaving the field was that they took away my rifle when I somewhat insulted when I explained that folk music in America was not "classical" music, which he quickly informed me was the case in China. Some of the students called their diplomas "working papers" and explained that they were interested in earning a degree so they could immigrate to the United States. But a few, like that lieutenant I shared a beer with back in August, planned to stick around to help their people.

Delighted, Doug—who been involved in the civil rights movement prior to the service—would shout out, "Hong Kong to the Hong Kongese!"

Doug was a CO who served in a hospital for POWs near Saigon. He spoke a little Vietnamese and told me that the NVA soldiers had a saying: "Three days." It meant that when the Americans left Vietnam, that's how long they thought it would take them to conquer the country. Based on my experiences with the ARVN and enemy troops, I told him I thought they just might be accurate in their prediction.

In 1969 Hong Kong was a city that thrived on American GIs. We were a boon to the economy. The Hong Kong dollar had an eight-to-one exchange rate with greenbacks, so we were instantly wealthy when we traded in our dollars. Doug bought an expensive movie camera. He was a former newspaperman like me, but now he was interested in other media. I bought a pair of prescription sunglasses, so that I would no longer squint on sweep, and a hand-tailored blue silk suit—a three-piece beauty in which I walked around barefoot, much to the amusement of the locals.

The Hong Kongese prostitutes made it their business to learn as much about the GIs as they could. One day as I was walking down the crowded boulevard in front of our hotel, a woman of the day grabbed me firmly in the crotch and said, "Hey Russell, how'd you like to have a good time like you used to back in Massachusetts."

I didn't know where she got her information, but I suspected Doug. He enjoyed visiting with the street people and quickly became a favorite of theirs, noncustomer though he was.

We were an odd couple, Doug and I, hiking around the thronging streets—him tall and gangly, good-naturedly singing the Beatles song "Black Bird"; me half a foot shorter, still wired from my long months of combat, and barefoot in a glossy blue suit.

As poor as my family had been when I was growing up, we had always had a home. I was amazed to learn that in Hong Kong people were born, lived their entire lives, then died, without ever having a home of their own other than a large cardboard box down some alleyway just off one of the busy streets. Meanwhile, from atop the bluff that looked out

went in. I never had a name for my M-16 the way some men n
cars or penises. After all these months, we had an understan
transcended words. If my rifle *did* have a name, it was Norman
at this point in my tour we were one. When I handed it ove
armorer in Tay Ninh, I felt a little like I was having an arm rippe
body. It was almost enough to make me want to stay in the field.
quite. Loyalty runs only so deep.

While I was standing on the airstrip at Cu Chi awaiting my fl
Ton Son Nhut, I had one of the most startling experiences of my
tour. Lynn Creel, my next-door neighbor in Indian Rocks Beach, h
off a plane. He was older than me, my brother's best friend in
school. We didn't have long to chat because my flight was rea
board, but what he told me left me chagrinned. Creel was the chief
of the entire 25th Division! He was the man who, in a very real se
ran the division. Had I arrived in Cu Chi a day earlier the previous
cember, I would have been working for him instead of humping the
der with Suicide Charlie.

Creel was returning from his sixth TDY to Singapore—essentially
all-expenses-paid vacation for which he was not charged tin
There but for fortune, I thought as I hopped my flight, consoled by tl
knowledge that I had only forty days to go. But I could not help bi
wonder how different my year might have been.

The trip to Ton Son Nhut was a dress rehearsal for the final journey
hoped soon to be making. That may have been why the army gave u
the leave, so we wouldn't arrive back in the States totally strange, utterl
unaccustomed to the ways of civilized society.

When I boarded the plane for Hong Kong, I took a seat next to a fel
low named Doug Ruhe. Doug was a bit like Phil and we hit it right off
He was a religious fellow, a Bahai, which he explained was a church tha
emphasized the spiritual unity of all people. That sounded good to me
as did his feelings about not frequenting brothels. We decided to share a
hotel room in Hong Kong and visit the city together.

We spent our days wandering the crowded colorful streets of the Brit-
ish colony, trying our best in the few days allowed to become familiar
with the people and their customs. We ate our lunches at the working-
class restaurants down by the docks, much to the amusement of the in-
digenous clientele. As I wrestled with chopsticks, spilling more rice than
reached my mouth, the unsophisticated locals would nudge their friends
and point to me, laughing and calling out encouragement.

One night we went to a folk concert at Hong Kong University and
struck up conversations with some of the students, the first of whom was

into the harbor, you could see fabulous towers of glass and steel as well as mansions where the wealthy lived, just blocks away from the destitute street people. It hardly seemed fair.

My favorite sight was the Kwoonloon Ferry. Several times a day it would motor across the harbor loaded with passengers. The moment it docked, thousands of businessmen—most so small compared to Americans that from the bluff they looked like boys playing grown-up, and each dressed in a three-piece suit and carrying a briefcase—would race off the boat to make their deals. Meanwhile, thousands more—identically dressed—would race on to go to the other side to complete their transactions. It was Wall Street in miniature, only at a far more furious pace, perhaps because failure there might mean returning to one of those boxes.

When our six days were over, I returned to Vietnam in a refreshed state of mind. Meeting Doug had affected my perspective on a lot of things, and I counted him an interesting new friend. As we were standing in line at Ton Son Nhut waiting to clear customs, I left him guarding my duffel bag while I went to the bathroom. When I returned, he was gone. The line had moved on and nobody knew what had happened to him. So I grabbed my bag, shrugged, and queued on through alone, accepting the odd way people popped in and out of other's lives in Vietnam. I spent one night at the Bien Hoa Repo Depot and then worked my way back to the field, my infantryman's cast of fatalism tinted with just a hint of anticipation.

I was very short. So short, as the saying went, that I had to climb a ladder to lace my combat boots.

Time—once my greatest enemy—was my ally now.

18

Time

The chaplain calls us together for a final briefing here in the bleachers at the Division HQ in Cu Chi. He speaks for only a few minutes of meaningless things: duty, honor, courage, and patriotism. They are code words for terror, sweat and grime, bugs and bullets. For endless days slogging through rice paddies and jungle. Noble words meant to cover the far darker reality of torn wasted lives, of bodies in pieces rotting in the sun and mouths frozen in perpetual screams.

Sorenson and I—he of the dead-body detail way back last Christmas—left our bunker in Tay Ninh and flew down this morning. We are just about out the door. We've got our gear in our duffel bags, our rifles in the armory, and we're ready for the Big Good-bye.

First thing we did when we came in from the field was add another layer of sandbags to our bunker. Charlie Company troopers to the end. But not Suicide Charlie anymore. We've lived down that name. Most of the group who shipped in by truck from Dau Tieng so many ages before will be going home. We have fought the battles, endured the campaign. We are Survivors.

"Your War is over," the chaplain intones. "Your nation will always be grateful. As you go on with your lives now, having met the test of battle in the proud tradition of American fighting men, there is just one thing that I want you to remember. When you get home, the people that you knew before you came here will seem different to you now."

Amen.

Everybody thinks they understand time. One second follows the next like soldiers marching in line. When sixty pass, that's a minute. Sixty more makes two. Time is a beautiful, straightforward, relentless progression. Tomorrow follows today, the future follows the present, which follows the past. Life unfolds in a time line, inexorably. The March of Progress. That's the way of the West.

In Vietnam it was different. We might have been living in a civilization before the very concept of time had been invented, so totally was time redefined for us. We had to learn the patience of the hunter and the hyper-alertedness of the hunted. The interminable pause, the unending hour.

There always seemed to be a moment, just before the shooting started, when it was silent and still and time hung suspended like a parachute flare snatched out of free fall and dangling, dropping slowly, slowly into the future. Then the fighting began and there was no time. The self disintegrated before a sensory overload of stimulation that opened a direct channel to the unconscious mind. We entered an instantaneous, timeless state.

The night of the battle of Mole City was the longest and shortest of my life. Time did not pass, it persisted. I remember the night as a blur but compressed within it was enough action and emotion to last a lifetime, a wild montage of flesh, flashes and phantoms suddenly turned still come morning.

There is no silence quite like that of a battlefield the morning after. It is the silence of spent emotion. All that remains is the rustle of the swaying leaves and the whispered mocking of the wind as it touches our folly and moves on, moves on.

The sun that rose over Mole City might have been rising over a Mesozoic plain ninety million years in the past for all that we had learned, for all that we had changed from the creatures of that era.

The concept of time, some might argue, is one of the great human developments that separates us from those primeval creatures. But noble a creation as it might be, in Vietnam chronological time was a boulder to push far heavier than the one Sisyphus pushed.

Each X on my short-timer's calendar represented a massive act of will. All day long I would fight back the compulsion to scratch away another day as if, by the ritual act of crossing it off my calendar, I would have lived it through. Time was an itch that would never stop; the best scratching occurred when, caught up in the war, several days passed with little notice. Out would come the calendar from its pocket of neglect and an orgy of X-ing would ensue. I gathered days in-country as a miser does dollars, and clung to them just as fiercely.

Time in-country was a form of wealth, in fact. The fewer days you had remaining, the greater was your fortune. Who could be more impoverished than a green FNG with 350 Days To Go. Better that he might be begging at a corner on the streets of the City of Joy than shuffling down the Highway of Tears outside Saigon on his way to a unit deep inside the war.

Sometimes we would bring out our calendars to show around like family albums, as if to say, "Here I am at two months in-country. What a handsome youth, callow still but coming along." Then four months later, "Look at me, strong and seasoned, turning the middle, rounding the bend, heading down the homestretch."

We were like racehorses on a one year oval, only the question was not who would finish first but who would finish, period.

The temptation always existed to cross out a few days ahead of time, just for the emotional charge. We were time-oholics, and each day was a shot from the bottle of Hard Times, 1968–69 being a particularly bad year. To mark out a day before it had ended was a grave sin, indeed. It omened ill. To take days before they were given was the most inexcusable indiscretion in the liturgy of time worship, like drinking wine before the chalice is blessed.

I struggled, as did all sincere penitents, to keep to the letter of my compact with the Great Purveyor of Passing Time, though at night— alone with my thoughts, my pen, and my calendar—my virtue was sorely tested.

Leave had given me a break from my time obsession but it was so brief, so fragile an illusion, that it had no staying power. As I journeyed back to Tay Ninh, I was reminded of my high school days when my family drove back to Florida at the end of summer. My leave memories broke apart like the signal from WBZ radio had, as I descended deeper and deeper into the War.

When I rejoined my unit, we were still pulling bushmasters under the new CO. I choppered out on a resupply drop, no longer the groovy dude barefoot in his three-piece suit, just another grunt with his ass on the line. But a short one.

The prescription sunglasses weren't much use on night ambush and they quickly disappeared, as all nonessentials did in Vietnam. We were carrying a heavy load, living out of our rucksacks for two weeks at a time, and my first priority was ammo, lots of it. I didn't want to run short if we popped an ambush way out there in the Angel's Wing. Fortunately, M-16 rounds are light because, as gunner, I was toting the tube and, more often than not, a round or two for the gun as well—rounds that the new ammo bearers seemed to discard with discouraging frequency.

We travelled mostly at night, humping thousands of meters in the pitch-black jungle darkness each time we relocated to a new ambush site. During the day, we lolled around waiting for the sun to finish its grand arc. If we were in an open area, we could strip off our clothing and dry out. The monsoon was heavy now, as we slipped deeper into October. A heavy rain beat on us all night long, seeping into our pores until the soft hidden parts of our bodies were red and raw and teeming with bacteria. One sunny day several days into a bushmaster, I stripped off my boots and socks and started counting sores that were creeping up from my toes to my knees. When I reached seventy-five and was barely above my left ankle, I quit in disgust. My body seemed to be disintegrating, rotting away until I would be like those half-cooked corpses I had dragged to the mass grave back at Mole City I.

The new CO was an interesting fellow, a Virginian with a bit of the Swamp Fox in him. As an ex–Green Beret, he was highly competent and well schooled in jungle lore. We were never ambushed while he was in charge. Chance may also have been a factor. During the rainy season, the war tended to slow way down, for obvious reasons.

The captain clearly enjoyed life in the bush, but there was a sad quality about him as well as the more obvious Boy Scout elan that he maintained on his surface. I found this dualistic quality interesting, and during the days when we were waiting around for a night movement I'd share lunch with him if I could. One day he told me about the Montagnards, the small aboriginal people who populated the Laotian hills where he had last been stationed as an advisor. It was clear that he admired these hardy resilient people who had become important allies, and what he said next was doubly shocking for that fact.

There were nearly fifty thousand tribesmen in his region when he first arrived there, he said. By the time he left, their numbers were down to less than five thousand. It wasn't the NVA that had killed them off, however, or the Pathet Lao, the Laotian communists. It was B-52 bombing raids that did them in, our CO said. Indiscriminate attacks supposedly aimed at NVA sanctuaries and supply routes. At that time, the American public had never even been informed that air strikes were occurring in Laos.

This information from my CO—a highly creditable firsthand account if there ever was one—fitted one more piece into the puzzle. We had decimated the very people who were aiding our airmen and harassing the enemy's supply lines! What kind of war was this that we were fighting? I had to wonder.

Each night as I waited in the darkness, unable to see more than a foot or two in front of me, I hoped that enemy soldiers would pass unnoticed, if any came by. What point was there to shoot them? Or for us to get shot by them? We were all in this together, I figured. The NVA, the Americans, and I. The real heavies, it seemed to me—if there were any in this absurd war—were the South Vietnamese, who didn't seem to want to fight for their own land, and the politicians on both sides, who were in it for glory, money, or power.

The NVA must have been thinking the same things because the better part of a month passed without us making any significant contact with the enemy. I had never expected to survive the War. October passed into November and the possibility that I *might* survive it became more and more real. But I was superstitious enough by that time to believe that fate might yet have one more trick up its sleeve. I was so superstitious, in fact, that I was wearing religious charms from every sect I could get my hands on: love beads, a soldier's cross, the entire ensemble. To an FNG, I probably looked a lot like Sergeant Miller had looked to me way back that previous December.

Unlike Miller, however, I hadn't flaunted the military in so outrageous a manner as to incur their undying animosity. I hadn't smoked pot in many, many months and I had always done whatever job had been assigned me. When I reached my last two weeks, my CO said I could take the next chopper back into Mole City II, lay low for a week, then head on in to Tay Ninh.

I'd been longing for this moment since the day I got my orders for Vietnam. If anticipation is a euphemism for anxiety, then I should have been a nervous wreck that final night in the field. But it wasn't exceptional in any manner. Just another dark rainy test of patience, waiting for the sun to rise.

When the sky brightened and the jungle vegetation regained its natural forms, we saddled up and started hiking to a clearing where we could await the resupply choppers. A few hours later we reached an appropriate spot—a large glade a couple football fields in area—and the CO radioed Tay Ninh. It was a clear hot day and some guys stripped down and went swimming in a couple bomb-crater pools placed there for our personal enjoyment by the B-52 landscape and recreation crew. I dropped my rucksack against a tree and laid back in the elephant grass, my steel pot tilted over my eyes and my feet up on a stump. The warm rays felt sweet as they burrowed into my damp clothing; puffs of steam rose up from my fatigue jacket as the sweat evaporated. The only downer in my idyll was my stomach: it was growling with hunger. I'd finished the last of my LRRPs the night before and they didn't stay with me, anyway. Reconstituted foods just don't make it over a long period of time.

With all the stuff I had been lugging, I couldn't handle much in the way of C-rations so I had stuck to freeze-dried LRRPs. Unfortunately, they lacked much in the way of real sustenance, and I got weaker and weaker the longer I stayed in the field. It didn't matter anymore, though. I was done.

As I was stretched out, word suddenly came down for everyone to take defensive positions. An enemy unit had been seen heading our way. Quietly, we took cover. The men in the pools snatched up their clothes and raced back naked while the rest of us hugged the earth, searching for any cover we could find, hiding in the tall grass that spiked up in thick clumps across the open field.

I peered down the barrel of my M-16, waiting. I didn't have to wait long. A few brown bodies flickered across the plain and we opened fire. Methodically, I sprayed the area before me with bullets, firing on semiautomatic to husband my ammo while I maintained dominance in my lane of fire.

The NVA soldiers fired back intermittently, caught by surprise and mainly interested in retreat. Bullets ripped through the tall grass and slammed into the trees to my rear. Our CO called in artillery and jet strikes, and explosions cratered the earth to our front. The enemy unit broke and, as suddenly as the firing began, it ended.

I was ordered to take my squad and sweep the area before us. Cautiously, we moved forward, spread out in a wide crescent. Across the clearing—less than a hundred meters away—the jungle began again, and somewhere within it the NVA soldiers had taken refuge. My only thought was to sweep the area as quickly as possible and get my men back out again before the survivors recovered from their shock.

We passed a few bodies, pausing only long enough to be certain they were dead, and continued on, concerned mainly about movement in the trees beyond. Our new platoon leader, Lieutenant Shuggs, stumbled across the body of a fallen soldier. Excited, he called us over to join him. It was his first sight of a corpse and he wanted to share it with us.

"Get over here," he shouted to me. "Check this out."

I ignored him totally, ordering my squad to keep moving, while he poked and prodded the body as if trying to comprehend something profound and unfathomable.

"Sergeant Russell," he called, this time more forcefully. "Come here. That's an order."

I waved him off with a flick of my wrist and kept on moving.

"Deserves a belly full of lead," I muttered to Pincush as we retreated to our original positions, relieved that either the NVA had fled or was too frightened to fire on us when we were in the open.

Chagrined, the lieutenant stalked back to our side of the clearing. What a fool, I could only think. Sergeant Meredith never would have endangered his men by taking time out for a freak show. The unit was changing and I was glad I was on my way out. There were too many new guys who had too little respect for the NVA. They didn't know what it was like to face a frontal assault, to fight through a night and wonder if dawn would ever break. They'd never faced the bravery of the toughest little soldiers God ever created, these fierce men in gray uniforms with the red insignias who marched in sandals for thousands of miles on a bowl of rice a day just to die in anonymity in the wire at some god-forsaken fire base.

If I'd had my way, we would have buried those bodies. They deserved it as much as we did.

Once our CO determined that the area was secure, he called in the choppers. He decided part of our unit should stay behind to search for any survivors of our ambush. Quietly, I slipped off toward the LZ, trying to look invisible. I was ready to leave. It didn't make sense for me to be there any more. My sympathies had become clouded. My sadness, my mourning, had come to embrace all of the dead, friend and foe alike. I had, in a way, truly become a universal soldier. I had fallen out of my culture, my time, and had become a creature of the earth, no longer just an American, no more a child of the twentieth century than of the first. I had entered a vast eternal realm in which all things were important, all lives mattered the same. I was, in a sense, mad, but I didn't know it yet.

I was just glad to be going home.

A few days later, I got the Big Nod. For some reason, Pincush was running a couple days behind me. I guess he'd made it through the repo depots a bit faster on his way out to the field. Sorenson was with me, though. He and I had never been very close. Maybe it was dragging all those decomposing bodies back at Christmastime. Not exactly the kind of experience that would bond one in an uplifting manner. For better or for worse, however, we were going home together. Nobody had to drag us with a rope and a rake. We were walking. No stretcher bearers, no body bags, no tin box with a few personal possessions.

We were taking eight-league strides in the boots we'd been reborn into as combat infantrymen. All I could think as I boarded one of those shaky C-47s in Cu Chi was that the Minister had misplaced our files.

The chaplain had those few words for us before we headed for the airstrip. I guess it hadn't occurred to him that it wasn't just our friends who had changed while we were gone. As I sat on the plane and watched the rice paddies disappear beneath me, and the tin and tarpaper shanties that filled the outskirts of Saigon began to appear, I felt an odd sense of disappointment. It all seemed so anticlimatic. I had achieved personal survival, but the war was not over. It didn't make sense, somehow, to be going home when the men of Suicide Charlie—strangers though many of them now might be—were still out there somewhere along the border, preparing for another long night sitting in the rain wondering if this was the night they came again.

When we reached Ton Son Nhut, the souvenir stands that had struck me as so hideous and mocking the Thanksgiving before now seemed merely ridiculous. I didn't bother to purchase a jacket.

While we were waiting in the lobby for the last manifest to be announced, I noticed a couple guys from AIT. They'd made it too. They were laughing and talking about the year they spent with the 9th Division down in the Mekong Delta. Not much had happened there. One fellow said it had been so quiet they'd seriously considered extending. Sorenson and I could only shake our heads. We were still wired from twelve months with Suicide Charlie.

"Different war, I guess," Sorenson commented, and I could only agree.

We weren't going to feel safe until we were thirty-five thousand feet up in the air, above the range of artillery rounds, for no fire was friendly.

After a while our names were called, and so—all those months and weeks and days since I had slipped onto that endless primordial plain once shared by dinosaurs, lemurs, and bolts of lightning, and I had become more like the grass and the wind than a man—I found myself, as if by a miracle, boarding a jetliner much like the one I had disembarked an eternity before. As I climbed the entry ramp and entered the cabin, I did not turn to wave.

The air was a delicious engineered cool, the stewardesses were young and beautiful, my seat was a deep cushion of softness that drew in my hard tired body, and sleep called me down.

It was a total sleep, deep and profound, a dreamless comatose sleep that marked my mental boundaries. I glided over South Vietnam and away, across Thailand, Guam, the mist enshrouded waters of the Pacific Ocean, leaving behind the American Troy and winging my way back to our modern-day Athens, the Garden of the West, lovely San Francisco.

When I awoke it was dark. The moon reflected across the black ocean, and stars sprinkled the sky.

For a moment I felt as if I was back out on night ambush. Only the comforting whine of the jet motors reminded me that I was encased in a metal womb, hurtling the distance from East to West, one reality to another. I looked around at my sleeping comrades who were dimly visible in the subdued light. They might have been dead and this plane an airborne crypt and I understood that we were all, in some silent unknowing way, marking a passage as strange and mysterious as the one from light into darkness that we had only delayed by surviving the War.

——— 19 ———

Life on the Border

"Now, what is the problem?" the nurse asks me, as she lays her hand across my forehead.

"I don't know," I reply. "It's strange. I feel weak, powdery, as if I am crumbling into dust."

More by chance than design I have wandered into the college infirmary. I was sitting in class when I suddenly felt as though I might collapse. This feeling of drifting, of fading away, is new and disturbing. For weeks I have been unable to sleep at night, such has been my anxiety. Now I am being affected in the daytime, as well.

"That's not much help," she says. "Can you be more specific."

"I think it has something to do with the War," I answer, surprised to hear myself say that. I've never made the connection before.

"The war?" she asks. "What war?"

"The Vietnam War. What other war would it be?"

"Yes, of course. I guess I'd forgotten."

"So had I," I reassure her. "I was an infantryman there, years ago. I don't know why but I think how I feel has something to do with that."

I got back from the War the same week the My Lai massacre was cover-story news in *Life* magazine, which may explain why people didn't want to talk much about it. Neither did I, actually. I just wanted to get on with life.

I did experience one kindness after my return. As it had been for the fellow who had been stood up by his wife in Hawaii, it was a stewardess who was responsible.

After a long night in San Francisco, turning in equipment, picking up leave pay from the quartermaster and such, I caught the early flight out of town. United Airlines, the Gourmet Special. I was flying half-price, military standby, in dress greens, and happy to have a cheap seat in the tourist section. Shortly after the plane roared down the runway, a stewardess came in and parked herself at the end of my row. She then announced to the handful of passengers there on the red-eye flight that tourist class was short one meal and somebody needed to move up to first. Nobody said a word, so I decided to take a chance and break the army's First Commandment—Thou Shalt Not Volunteer.

She led me up front and I took a window seat. A waiter wheeled out the fanciest cart of victuals I had ever seen. It overflowed with prime rib, shrimp, roast beef, a dozen different types of liqueurs. Now I understood why this flight was called the Gourmet Special. I ate and drank until I passed out from satiation and didn't awaken until I was in Hartford several hours later.

I had a month to kill in Greenfield before I had to report to Fort Carson, Colorado, to finish out my two years. It didn't make much sense, having to return to the army now that the war was over for me. The prospect of Stateside duty was why Lopez had extended, but I didn't regret my decision not to, despite the extra time in uniform. Just being alive was reward enough.

It had to be. Other than the generosity of the stewardess, being a veteran didn't amount to much in December 1969. That and a quarter, as the saying went, would buy you a cup of coffee.

I spent my month back at the paper. The *Recorder* had been unlucky in their replacements for me, and the sports department was in disarray. So I picked up right where I left off: a desk, a phone, and a byline. It was an odd sensation, almost as if my interlude in Vietnam were just that—a brief sidestep out of ordinary life, a window to another world that had opened and closed and reopened again.

I did have a little problem with the editor, however. My tolerance for taking orders was rather limited and, on those occasions when he attempted to assert some authority over me, I was quick with the rebuke.

"I'm the sergeant here, not you," I recall growling at him one morning. He left me alone after that, remembering, perhaps, how he had felt when he returned home after infantry duty in Europe during World War II.

When the first of the year rolled around, I caught a flight out to Colorado Springs for the final 150 days. The cruelest thing about the experience was the way they made us stand in formation every morning at the repo depot. A cold snap hit the base just about the time I arrived. Like most of the other guys back from Vietnam, I had spent a year in the tropics preceded by several months at a southern training base and all I had were summer clothes. The thermometer dipped to 20° below a few mornings, and the army—being compassionate by nature if not design—finally relented and allowed us to wear civilian sweaters under our thin dress greens. By then, I and many other new arrivals had severe bronchitis, of course, but our discomfort and ill health were small prices to pay for maintaining the sanctity of the military dress code.

It took a week or so of shopping around before I found a unit willing to take me. Short Round, it turned out, had become a battalion Ex-O. He was a captain now. He recognized my name and signed me on as a public relations NCO. Now I really *was* going to write for a base newspaper.

There was not much heavy lifting involved in my new position. My main job was writing PR releases for the hometown papers of men whose Vietnam-won decorations were just coming through. I also had to operate the battalion mimeograph machine. As a sergeant, I didn't have to pull details.

I soon learned that the primary mission of my battalion was riot control in the northern Midwest. Apparently, government officials were terrified that college students in Pierre, South Dakota, might hatch a plot to overthrow the United States.

Right on, I thought, and I let it be known where my sympathies would lie in such an unlikely eventuality. My battalion sergeant major—a pipe-smoking grandfatherly gent with graying hair and a dignified mien more professorial than military—enjoyed taunting me with a huge pair of scissors that he kept on his desk. He told me he would make me use them to cut the hippies' hair, ensuring my compliance with a bayonet in my back. It was black humor at its darkest—an army staple. Unfortunately, I couldn't appreciate it to its fullest extent. Depression had begun to bring me down.

One day the sergeant major took me aside and dropped his arm across my shoulders. He had seen three wars and knew the signs of postcombat depression. Not that it took the insight of Freud to pick them out. After a month in Fort Carson, I had begun to have trouble getting out of my bunk in the morning for reveille. I would stagger out to formation without bothering to lace my boots so as to save time when I hopped back into bed again. Eating became a great effort, as did taking showers, brushing my teeth, all the petty activities of everyday life.

"Russell," the sergeant major told me, "your problem is that you don't forget well enough."

He was right. My depression was a direct result of trying to shut off that part of my brain that had been so affected by the war, and it wasn't working too well. Finally, I realized that I once again was suffering from a personal problem and went to see the chaplain.

This time it was different. He listened. And I poured my heart out. Driven by a wildfire of emotions and memories suppressed for these many months, my words stampeded forth until all of my despair was spent and I could no longer speak, but merely sob like a child. When I had calmed down, he made a few phone calls that led to a month's convalescent leave.

Elated, and packing a small vial of Librium, I returned to Greenfield and signed up for the spring term at the community college I had so briefly attended two years before. My plan was to try for a college enrollment early release from active duty, or early-out, when I returned to Fort Carson. Suddenly I was a student instead of a soldier!

It didn't work. The circumstance was a unique one because, when I filed for the early-out, I was already enrolled and had been attending classes. That threw the bureaucracy for a loop, and by the time it was untangled it was too far into the semester for me to return. Just the thought of getting out had sustained me over those first crucial weeks, however, so that by the time the situation had been resolved negatively, I only had about three months left in my hitch. It was spring, the war had backed off a bit, and the sky brightened.

Had I not been so keyed up at the outset, I would have realized that, basically, as far as we returning combat vets went, nobody at Fort Carson gave a damn as to what our attitude was as long as we didn't get in the way. The army had as little use for us as we did for them. Riot duty was mostly just a straw dog so we'd have something to kick at and the military could justify the expense of maintaining thousands of soldiers for a few months more.

Once I caught on, I bought a motorcycle and moved off base. It was against the regulations but, as long as I made it in on time for duty each morning, nobody gave a damn. Next thing I knew, I met a woman named Connie at a "head shop" where she sold leather goods and drug paraphernalia. She was pretty, intelligent, and very short. She also liked motorcycles, so she bought a pair of size-one boys' motorcycle boots and we started cruising.

Connie was a member of what passed for the Colorado Springs "counterculture" in the spring of 1970, and she shared an apartment with two gay men. Soon I moved in with them, forming an unlikely quartet. Each night, the older of the two men would bid me good-night with a heart-felt "Sweet dreams, beautiful." I didn't really mind because he was a macho little dude who'd done his time as an airborne ranger during the Korean War.

"I wasn't going to let them think that just because I was a queer meant that I was a fairy," he confided in me, taking pride in the distinction.

If only I'd known him when we were jogging along in Basic, singing the Airborne Ranger song. It would have put that jingle in an entirely different perspective.

I liked Connie, and her friends, but not enough to stay in Colorado when my hitch was up. The morning of June 19, 1970, I left the base and pulled up to a stop sign on my bike. I was young, strong; I had several hundred dollars in my wallet and discharge papers in my pocket. This was the moment the thought of which had enlivened my spirit for two years. I was free, white, twenty-one, and under no yoke. The paper had found a suitable replacement for me, so I had no job. Kelly and I had cut it clean, so I had no one waiting for me at home. I sat at the stop sign, gunning my motor, clutch in, wondering which way to turn.

It is to avoid such moments that some men do crazy things the last few weeks of their enlistments, such as marrying a girl they have known for only a few weeks or, worse yet, re-upping.

Neither thought ever entered my mind.

A wiser man than I was might have taken Horace Greeley's advice of a century before and gone west. But it was a sunny June morning not un-like the one two years previous when I had set out to hitchhike to Florida for induction, and sheer momentum pushed me east to complete the cycle and return to where it all began.

I have Mohawk Indian blood in my veins and the spirit of my ances-tors does linger in my soul. There is one small county in western Massa-chusetts outside of which I have never felt totally comfortable.

The best part of getting out of the service was the ride home. For two weeks, I fell out of the world. After a few days, I found myself wishing that the journey would never end. In a sense, of course, it never has.

The one reminder of the war came at a bar in Pennsylvania, where a Canadian man bought me a beer in gratitude for my not fleeing to his country to avoid the draft.

I received no similarly generous offers from the Americans I met.

For the lack of anything better to do, I spent the summer in Greenfield, hanging out and collecting unemployment. I considered school in the fall, but I wasn't ready. Connie came out for a visit and I toyed with the idea of returning to Colorado with her, but it wasn't in the cards. Finally I enrolled at the community college for the spring semester of 1971.

That spring the antiwar movement really came of age. Just before I had mustered out at Fort Carson, Nixon had launched the invasion of Cambodia, his last desperate act to rescue a failing South Vietnamese Army. His secret plan had turned out to be "Vietnamization" of the war—in other words turning it over to the Marvin the ARVNs and Ruff Puffs we had had the mischance of seeing in action. Perhaps if "Tricky Dick" had done a little time on the line he would have realized how futile this program would be and why the NVA POWs had told Doug, "Three days."

The invaders went in right through our zone, trying to finish up the job we started at Frontier City. They were going after COSVN, the legendary Southern Command HQ of the NVA, but they never found it. Still, I was impressed by the importance Command put on the place. We went in with one hundred men; this time they sent ten thousand.

Reaction to the invasion of Cambodia (Nixon called it an "incursion") was predictably strident. We never got sent to Pierre, but the governor of Ohio did make the mistake of allowing his National Guard troops to carry loaded weapons at Kent State University and they did what one would expect from a bunch of weekend warriors—losing their cool and shooting four antiwar protestors on May 4, 1970. A lot of the excitement slipped by me those last few weeks of my enlistment. I just wanted to ride my bike, get high, and go home. But the following year—student now that I was—I joined in the antiwar protests when many of my classmates decided to drive to Washington to express their patriotic dissent.

I was never into the rhetoric all that much, but I enjoyed the ambience of the demonstrations. There was an exuberance to the antiwar people that paralleled mine, as well as a lively touch of anarchy. Excited as I was simply to have survived the war, I found it easy to relate to the enthusiasm of the young protestors.

Later that spring, when the Vietnam Veterans Against the War (VVAW) decided to march from Concord Bridge to Bunker Hill, retracing the steps of the Minutemen who fired the "shot heard 'round the world" that marked the beginning of the American Revolution, I joined in for the hike.

We were arrested in Lexington for breaking the town park ordinance and loaded onto buses for an overnight in the DPW garage, but even that turned into a party as hundreds of town citizens demonstrated their support for our action by joining us in our temporary cell, supplying us with food, and paying our fines the next morning. For once, being a Vietnam veteran paid off.

I emerged from that immediate postwar phase of my life married, with a two-year degree and a scholarship to Amherst College. Life looked good. Despite occasional setbacks, I could envision a future that involved a career, family, success in all the conventional activities society weighs most significant. But it was not to be. That thing that broke the summer of '69 had yet to be repaired. By the fall of 1974, I found myself slipping in all ways, my marriage was in a state of collapse, I couldn't concentrate on schoolwork, eventually I couldn't even sleep.

Where once I had believed that I had left the War far behind, now I was to learn that my real battle had only just begun.

I began to believe that if I fell asleep, my lungs would stop working and I would suffocate. Sleep had come to mean death to me. And for a very good reason.

When I slept, I dreamed. And when I dreamed, I was back in the war. For months I lay at night in a twilight of consciousness while cartoonlike illusions passed before my eyes—two-dimensional dreams that offered no release. There came a time when death itself would have been a not unpleasant release, but I did not yield to the temptation as my father had. Perhaps it was simple obstinacy—the determination that I had survived Vietnam and I wasn't about to give up now.

My marriage ended. College, of course, was lost. At night, the dark part of my mind began to make pictures that murdered my soul. In my dreams, I was always on the border. Sometimes my rifle jammed as a wave of NVA soldiers crashed down on me. In other dreams, the barrel of my gun melted or my weapon simply disappeared as an enemy soldier pointed his rifle to my temple and pulled the trigger. One recurring nightmare found me fleeing a broken burning city, pushing women and children before me into the deep pulsating darkness while NVA fighters danced like puppets amidst bonfires. They pursued me across streams and mountains, through jungle and plain, relentless human bloodhounds who never lost scent of my trail.

Eventually I fell out of society entirely, taking up residence in a communal home where I could survive on only a few dollars a month. I had no car, no regular job, just a room with a bed, a bottle, and a memory.

One night after going out dancing and drinking far too much, I found myself stumbling down a dark highway. I had argued with my friends, convinced that they were driving in the wrong direction, and jumped from the auto when they wouldn't turn it around. As I walked deeper into the deserted countryside along the back road, I eventually had to admit that I had been wrong once more. This was not the first time I had found myself in such an embarrassing position and, when I reached a main road where I could phone for a ride, I swore that I would never find myself in this situation again, going the wrong way down the road of life. Though it was very late and far out of their way, some of my housemates came and picked me up. As I rode home, I understood a little bit more about the positive aspect of people: that although humans are capable of great evils, as I had witnessed in Vietnam, they are also capable of kindnesses, small as well as large, and they can forgive.

Society had a strong interest in putting the War behind it, as did we veterans. Nobody likes to lose and, as Seneca once wrote, after a war nobody asks if it was right or wrong, just who won.

Vietnam veterans, in many ways, became pariahs, outcasts to the very people who voted to send them to War in the first place. The same citizens who overwhelmingly reelected Nixon president in 1972 cheered as he was driven from office two years later and sat in silent judgment when the NVA POWs promise to Doug Ruhe of "three days" became a reality in the spring of 1975.

I felt an odd mixture of relief and despair when the war finally ended. But for the South Vietnamese who fled, I felt only disdain. Had they been willing to fight, the War would have ended long before. I couldn't imagine an American unit routed as were their units, and my judgment was harsh. Fair-minded? Perhaps not, but that's the way I saw it at the time.

I began my homefront personal "counteroffensive" to regain respect for Vietnam veterans on Veterans Day of the same year by posting a sign on the bulletin board of my communal home that read: "Support your house veteran—Take a veteran out to lunch."

One of my housemates, Donald Boy, whose father had been a career officer in the army, took me up on my suggestion. For the first time since that Canadian stood me a drink in a bar in Pennsylvania, my discharge paid a dividend. That free meal tasted sweet and began a tradition that Donald maintained for several years. It marked a humble beginning to my campaign, but it was a start and that's all that counted.

The following year I returned to college and gradually remerged with society. At twenty-nine, I felt like an old man among children—most of my fellow students had still been in grade school while I was fighting for my life in Vietnam—but I ran the course and earned my degree in the spring of 1980. It had been a long journey and, though my past in many ways still haunted me, I now had a stake in the future, embodied in the tiny form of a baby boy named Shannon.

20

Lessons of Peace

A light snow drifts down from the scalloped March sky. The chill breeze stiffens my naked fingers as I toss my line into the river, but all around me I see signs of spring. Fragments of ice skitter past on the swollen water, grey-yellow junkos leap from branch to branch of maples and oaks that blush red with fattening buds. Far across the stubble-spiked pasture I hear a morning dove calling to the rising sun.

The fish that survived the winter beneath the frozen water are swift and hungry. Their quick dark shadows dart from rock to rock, reminding me of the soldiers passing through the wire at Mole City on their way out to night ambush. Battling the current, they flit upstream where the early torrent has chewed into the awakening earth, releasing worms and larvae.

Crystals of hoarfrost sparkle silver in the early sunlight that slants down as the clouds break along the horizon. I feel the warming rays burrowing into my neck and shoulders as I wait, hunched over my pole, alert for the snap of the line if a trout hits my baited hook.

Just upstream, around a bend, I see the fuzzy top of Shannon's wool cap bobbing amid the bankside brush.

"I think I've got one!" he calls.

Setting my pole on a rock, I hurry over to give him a hand. A glossy fingerling tosses in the air and slaps against the water. Together we reel it in. Shannon's first catch of the season.

Proudly, he holds it high. The small fish shudders and sparkles, its bulging eyes quivering in terror with a look that I have seen before. Gently I pull out the hook and place the fish in Shannon's palm.

"It is so little," I say. "I think you should throw it back in."

Disappointment tugs at his excitement briefly as he holds it tight. Then he carries it down to the water's edge.

"You're right, Dad," he says firmly. "It needs time to grow big, just like me."

He slips it into a shallow eddy. The trout hesitates for a moment, regaining its balance, then flits off into deeper water. Tears form at the edges of my eyes and, looking back, Shannon senses my sadness.

"It's OK, Dad," he says softly, moving close and snuggling his small hand into mine. "I'll catch it again for you later."

For a few minutes we stand together, holding hands and silently watching the rushing stream. The dark water is a mirror and in it I can see many things. The cold makes Shannon begin to shiver and we gather up our gear, climb up the banking to Creamery Road, and walk slowly back home.

When the sound of the torrent has abated and the exercise has warmed our bones, Shannon tugs on my hand and looks up at me.

"Why were you crying, Dad?" he asks, always the questioner, always the one with the courage to seek wisdom.

"There was a boy, once, a long, long time ago," I reply, cautious with my words, not quite sure how to answer. "He got caught in some bushes. I wanted to let him go."

During AIT, our platoon sergeant—a large Filipino we called Sergeant Tad—confided to us one day that he had been scared as hell when he first got to Vietnam. Then, he explained, he realized that he had the power to kill and his fear disappeared.

"Half the power of God," he said, the words rolling across his lips like a fat Havana cigar.

Then he spat bullet sounds from between his teeth, whirling about as if to fire in all directions like a mad caricature of Sergeant York, spraying our barracks with frenzied bursts of pretend machine-gun fire.

While I never did share his enthusiasm for slaughter, I too learned the power of an automatic weapon. It was a hard lesson to forget. Though my main weapon was a mortar, I carried an M-16 at all times and used it with intent more than once. My rifle was the weapon I ultimately depended on, the one essential item of equipment. Without it in my hands or nearby I felt awkward, as if naked in a public place. When I tucked it under my arm, my finger on the trigger as we marched along on sweep, I could feel its potency and came to know, as Sergeant Tad had said I would, what it was like to command half the power of God.

There are things a young man in civilized society should never know and one of them is how it feels to hold an automatic weapon in his grasp, his finger taut against the smooth steel trigger, as it pours fire toward another man's belly. Certainly I wish *I* had never known.

I've never touched a weapon since I've been out of uniform. For me, a rifle has only one purpose and that is to kill other men—boys, sometimes. Certainly there were occasions when, frustrated by some asshole or other, I wished I had back my old M-16, locked and loaded, just to see the stunned look of terror that would grip his smug features as a burst of rounds sprayed into his stomach. Maybe that's why I've stayed away from weapons. The temptation might be too real.

Combat veterans carry a unique burden. They are aware of their capacity for violence. Many have turned that violence in on themselves. It is said that twice as many Vietnam veterans have died at their own hands than died from those of the enemy. So far, I have been able to count myself among the fortunate ones who managed to find a spark of hope amid the ashes of war.

When my first son, Shannon, was born, I stood beside his mother, Sharon, and saw the look that leaped between their eyes as mother and infant were reunited by the doctor. An electric charge surged between them and I knew it for what it was, a soul-piercing flash of recognition such as that I had shared with a wounded child over ten years before.

Truly, I was born again at that moment of deliverance as I experienced the other half of God's power: the power to create. Shannon's birth was a miracle, but a desperate one that almost ended in the ultimate despair, for he was born prematurely by seven or eight weeks and his lungs did not work.

His illness was called "hylen membrane disease," today easily curable but at the time only conquered by an act of God, with a small assist from medical science. His body had to learn how to produce surfactin, the substance that coats the lining of our lung cells so that they are not brittle and can exchange gases properly.

It was as grim a scene as any pre-attack meeting at HQ when we sat in late-night conference with two doctors the day he was born and they told Sharon and me that Shannon had to learn how to breathe on his own within ninety-six hours or he would die. They could purchase that much time with technology, and no more.

Hour after hour I sat by his incubator, watching helplessly as he hyperventilated, fighting for his life with every ounce of his tiny emaciated body that became more and more gaunt. The precious ounces melted away as I waited, sometimes reaching into the incubator and laying my hand across his heaving chest so he would not feel alone in his struggle.

In all my life, I had never felt such agony. Surely, if it would have made the difference, I would have given my life to save his.

On his miniature wrinkled shoulders, Shannon was carrying a double burden—his life and mine—for he was not going to leave this world alone. Inside his transparent glowing box he was an angel of life, or an angel of death; only time could tell which.

Well into the third day I thought I detected a change in his breathing. I had been watching him the way we used to stare out at the wire at the French Fort, and I didn't know if what I was seeing was real or an apparition. I called the nurse over for verification, and we shared my exaltation.

Shannon could breathe on his own!

It was a few weeks before he could come home to our apartment. There was lost weight to be regained and progress to be monitored, but he was a large baby as premies go, and healthy once his lungs started to work. I returned to my university studies a new man. Shannon's birth had been a biological event of such power that it changed the very fabric of my being, as if every cell in my body had been altered, the chemicals of despair supplanted by those of hope. I had waited ten years for that change to occur, and now I understood a profound lesson of peace: that humankind has been touched by the hand of God, and the Promethean gift we have received can be used to create and nurture life as well as to destroy it. War, in all its horror, had taught me to abhor technology. Neonatal science and Shannon's salvation had reminded me in undeniable terms that the evil comes not from God but from Man.

With the birth of Shannon, I faced a new challenge, that of setting aside the anger that had come, in many ways, to dominate my life—anger at the society that had sent me off to be killed, and to kill, anger at a nation that seemed to hold us Vietnam veterans in such low esteem, anger at myself for failing in marriage, in school, in so many ways when delayed stress interrupted my life.

Anger, it might be said, is the shadow of pain. I had been hurt in many many ways. The World War II combat veterans had experienced the horror of war but they, at least, had the assurance of knowing that their cause had been just. Society had honored their service, and most had repressed their memories and maintained the code of silence that protected them against their pain. For us Vietnam vets the situation was far more ambiguous.

We had witnessed a nation destroyed, had seen soldiers and civilians alike die in agony for a cause that was at best dubious. To move beyond the anger, the rage, that threatened yet to ruin my life meant expiating the pain, and the price of atonement is self-awareness.

One day I watched on TV an interview with the Argentinean journalist Jacobo Timerman, who had been "disappeared" and tortured by the military junta who ruled that country during the 1970s. Timerman said that he had delayed undergoing psychiatric counseling after his release from prison for the sake of the memory of his fellow inmates who had been tortured and murdered.

"I have a loyalty to the pain," Timerman said to his interviewer and I knew exactly what he meant.

It was the boy whose pain it was hardest to forsake. I had carried his agony within for so long that it truly had become a part of me. How deeply it had settled within my soul I was not aware for many years because I had totally repressed the memory of him.

One afternoon not too long after Shannon was born, I was sitting on the steps of a friend's quiet country home, sipping whiskey and talking about things, when he asked me about the War. Suddenly, the memory of that boy surged up through my unconscious as if the alcohol had opened a channel into my past and I found myself crawling across the lawn, reenacting that terrible scene at the clump of bushes along the Cambodian border. Sobbing, I shouted out the horrible details to my stunned host. I could see the boy, feel his wounds, share his agony as our souls met and embraced, and then it was over. A portion of my rage dissipated, vanishing like smoke into darkness. As I walked home to Sharon and Shannon and our small apartment, I knew that part of my war had ended. I had replaced that dead child with one of my own, and it was time to move on in life.

Knowing and doing are two different things, however, and the twin toxins of alcohol and rage still threatened this new life I had created. I knew that I, like Timerman, needed counseling if I was ever to fully heal from the wounds of war. Not long afterwards, I went to the Veterans Administration for assistance. For years I had avoided this stage of readjustment, in part out of fear. My country had tried to kill me once, the paranoid aspect of my mind that first emerged at the French Fort reasoned. Given a second chance surely it would not fail to finish the job.

Only my commitment to my family gave me the courage to make this next step. I knew that if I did not receive some form of psychological assistance, I would eventually drive Sharon and Shannon away from myself. I might even follow the footsteps of my father up those long dark stairs. Suicide Charlie, I knew, was more than just a catchy nickname. It was a metaphor for my life.

Ironically, my first visit to the VA led to the rejection of my plea for help. Delayed stress had not yet been recognized as an official psychiatric condition. It was determined that I suffered from "failure to adjust to adult life." This struck me as ridiculous. I had adjusted well to adult life. I had graduated from high school, started a career in journalism, fulfilled my military commitment while gaining the rank of sergeant, even had a good-conduct ribbon, and was well on my way to a college diploma.

Life should have been fine, but instead there was this aching in my heart that would not let me rest. Something more had to be involved than a failure to adjust to adult life!

After I developed an ulcer I returned to the VA for treatment and, this time, found a counselor who had taken to heart the cause of Vietnam veterans. Richard Sette, though not a combat vet himself, cared about my problems and those of other men like me. In his small office I came to understand that my experiences in the war were important and held great personal significance. Rather than discrediting those experiences, as much of society had seemed determined to do, he helped me explore and come to terms with them.

The trauma, the survivor's guilt questioning why you lived when so many others died, the psychic numbing that crippled emotions and led to outbursts of rage, the nightmares that were a pathway to the unconscious haunting ground of repressed memories—gradually, with Sette's assistance, I began to put words to these and other conditions that had effectively blocked my emotional development just as I should have been emerging into full maturity.

I was only twenty the night I first heard the Devil scream at Mole City, and still that young when I had passed spark with the boy. So much of what I had experienced in Vietnam was so totally different from anything else I had ever known before that I really had no way of rationalizing it at the time. Some events, such as dragging the bodies after they began decomposing, were so disturbing that they caused me to form distinct personalities to deal with them, just as happens in the case of victims of child abuse. This, I believe, is the source of flashbacks. An actual shifting into a different, normally repressed personality.

The counseling at times was so painful that I found myself doubting the sincerity of Sette. Was he not, after all, an agent of the government that had created my torment. Paranoia, my old friend, came to visit me again. One day, as I was driving in for a counseling session, I was seized by the conviction—as powerful as had been those when I had been ducking imaginary rounds at the French Fort—that this was how they were going to "eliminate" me. I knew it was mad and I struggled to control my fear. As I walked into his office, I was fighting down an almost uncontrollable urge to flee to the woods and hide, as many veterans have and remain trapped there even today.

After I sat down, another man came in. He and Sette held a whispered conversation of which I heard only the last few words.

"I'll meet you upstairs in fifteen minutes."

This is it, I thought, gripping the arms of my chair, forcing myself to remain seated even though I was certain they were going to take me upstairs, for what? We talked briefly, then Sette excused himself. I waited, terrified, until he returned and completed our scheduled hour. When it ended, I found that I was free to leave! My paranoia vaporized. It had been betrayed by reality. It was then that I knew that the worst of my troubles were over.

Learning to live with peace is a never-ending struggle for those who have been traumatized by war. Many years were wasted and many of us have fallen far behind those of our generation who did not serve in combat. Counseling could not erase the fact that I had no career and no home of my own. While understanding can help rationalize past experiences, war memories do linger.

Late at night, when the winds are high and the moon darts in and out of swiftly moving clouds, there are times when I can still hear the voice of the Devil screaming just as he did the night I made his acquaintance. I was an infantryman—and no counseling, no education or readjustment program, can ever change that.

The dark still comes. The night still moves. The Minister of Misery yet holds my file. Maybe someday, as Stan suggested, I will drink that quart of bourbon and go out and ask him who won. Then I'll get my chance to find out if I, like Sergeant Miller who fought so valiantly at Mole City, can look him straight in the eye, spit in his face, and smile when I call him asshole.

Epilogue

Over the years I gradually gathered together bits and pieces of what happened to my father. With five children he was draft exempt, but he volunteered because he believed that World War II would mean the end of war if the Allies won. He didn't want his sons to have to fight.

According to one of my brothers, he served with General Patton, had a truck blown out from under him, and suffered from head injuries. Then he was shipped back to England where he served on an anti-aircraft battery. One night a plane carrying two dozen American troops failed to identify itself and was shot down by his battery, killing everyone on board.

When he returned from overseas, the memory of the incident haunted him. He also suffered from terrible headaches, perhaps as a result of the head injuries. When the Cold War began, he came to realize that, far from ending warfare, World War II had created a situation in which future conflicts appeared to be inevitable. This realization depressed him terribly, destroying, as it must have, his rationale for enlisting. His depression intensified until, finally, he made that last solitary journey up to the attic.

Ironically, he had sought a job as a printer at the Greenfield *Recorder* ever since returning from overseas and had finally gotten one just a few weeks before he died. His short tenure there may be why no one in the editorial department remembered him.

Though our wars were very different and the reasons we served quite different as well, I do feel that my experiences as an infantryman have helped me to understand why he chose to take his own life. Any person who is near the death and destruction of the battlefield for long cannot fail to recognize the vast power embodied in the dark side of human nature. For an idealist, as I assume my father was, comprehending the human capacity for evil presents a terrible threat to one's sense of purpose in life.

Perhaps, under different circumstances, my father could have learned to live with the knowledge he gained in Europe, but his age may have conspired against him. Youth, at least, has the advantage of sheer physical energy. The biological drive to live is very strong at 21.

At 44, I have now outlived my father by six years. No longer do I feel fated to follow in his footsteps. Time has proven otherwise, and for that I am grateful. Such is not the case for many Vietnam veterans, however. It is said that well over twice as many of them have committed suicide since the war than soldiers died in Vietnam. It is harder to imagine a more damning testimonial to the tragic nature of the combat experience.

The legacy of the War continues to affect many, if not all, of the members of the Vietnam generation. Few were not touched by the War in some fashion or other. Reports that we, as a society, have finally put the Vietnam War behind us are greatly exaggerated. I hope we never do. To me the true lesson of Vietnam, and any conflict involving civilized people, is that every life counts, each single human being matters. I firmly believe that combat veterans are uniquely qualified to affirm this principle, and I hope that in some small way my book may add to the dialogue concerning war and encourage other veterans to break the fraternity of silence that united the veterans of World War II. It is only through our voices that the memory of the pain, anguish, and despair of combat can be kept real.

As the mania that swept the United States during the war in the Persian Gulf demonstrated, it is only too easy to forget the humanity of the soldiers on both sides of the wire. Many of the Iraqi troops who were buried alive after being pounded senseless by a month of unrelenting B-52 bombing attacks were boys just like myself when I was at Mole City or Frontier City. Their fatal sin was that their military lacked air superiority.

Much like my father, I hope fervently that my sons, Shannon and Nathaniel, shall never have to undergo the terrible experiences that I did during a time that now seems so long, long ago. As for my dad, that veteran who chose silence, I can now forgive him as I could not during those distant days when I was a child and the shadow of his suicide darkened my life. I wanted so badly to know him, to feel his touch, to speak with him. Someday, I am certain, he and I shall finally meet. Until then I can best speak to him through a poem that I wrote at a time when my children were very young and I was struggling so desperately to deal with the legacy of his death and that of the War.

FATHERS AND SONS

When you raced across Europe with Patton
through shattered hamlets and ruined towns,
quiet in death;
When Cities trembled beneath sheets of bombers
that cloaked the sky
in a shroud of revenge;
When life fled the bodies of men
from a hundred nations,
And a generation of children wandered,
fatherless,
through rubble piles,
across cratered streets,
and huddled against jagged toothed tenement walls,
wrapped in rags
as the bitter Northern winter
bit into their sallow flesh
like wild packs of starving dogs;

When German carbines
slammed bolt against brass,
and dotted the night in sparkles;
And German artillery
tore bone from bone,
As you raced deep into the Eastern fortress
on that furious chase
into the heart of Evil;

Did time break into pieces,
like clouds at dawn,
as heat layered upon heat,
until the sun burst,
and blindness sank down through you,
followed by
What?

I knew you only as
mystery.
And you, me, not at all.

Would you have held me
and told me,
things a boy needs to know,
of mercy,
of kindness,
of time and of bodies,
melting like snow.

And on drives through the country,
on long Saturday afternoons,
of work, faith, and women,
driveshafts and wheels,
and how to drink whiskey,
and how men make steel,
Or why I wake,
trembling,
in my 35th year,
When my dreams are of blood,
black powder,
and fear;
And what's real seems illusion,
and memory breaks real
across the dark part of my mind that
makes pictures,
that murder my soul.

I go to my son,
and lie at his side,
to bathe in life's promise
and take courage from his sleep,
trusting the serene
strength of his smile,
as he feels me near.

Fathers without sons,
sons without fathers,
This cycle of pain,
Is the mesage of War.

The message is insane
that I learned in the jungles of South Vietnam,
And you, in your own time,
on the European plain.

I watch my son sleeping
and I vow:
Not him, not again.
No, not him.

We will take those Saturday rides,
build houses in trees and fish by the stream,
Talk about whiskey, women, and things,
Hike in the mountains and hear the grass sing.
I will teach him about crankshafts,
and how men make steel,
How to hit the fastball, an overhand curve,
How to carve figures
from a fine stock of ash.

Fathers and sons,
sons and fathers,
I pray:
Lord, grant us time,
That we may know one another.

And I return to my room,
to wait out the dawn,
to sweat out the terror,
and swallow the pain,
That I might be here
come morning
When my son awakens to wonder
and calls out my name.

Author's Note

Though this story reads much like a novel, it is a true one. What happened, happened pretty much as it is depicted, to the best of my memory.

The people are real. I did not change the names of the characters, as is oftentimes done in books such as this, because I respect too greatly the people with whom I served to render them into anonymity. I hope they don't mind.

What dialogue the story contains is re-created in the spirit of the people who speak. As Paul Fussell, author of *Wartime*, has suggested, there is an inverse relationship between the veracity of a war memoir and the amount of dialogue. Though some remarks ring true with the clarity of certitude, it would be arrogant to suggest that I can remember exactly what everyone said almost twenty-five years ago.

The soldiers of Suicide Charlie were young men forced to deal almost daily with situations that would test the wisdom of the greatest philosophers. If sometimes we seemed silly and immature, if occasionally judgment lapsed before expedience, it is because we were only kids. We just didn't know it at the time.

The true miracle is that we comported ourselves so well—even nobly—under such difficult circumstances. Much suffering throughout Southeast Asia and the United States might have been averted if only the leaders of our nation could have done the same.

About the Author

NORMAN L. RUSSELL is a graduate of the University of Massachusetts and a self-employed writer. He has written and produced a PBS TV program entitled *Fathers and Sons: Two Generations of American Combat Veterans*, which won numerous awards.